Vocabulary Puzzles

The Fun Way to Ace Standardized Tests

John T. Molloy and Rich Norris

BICENTENNIAL
1807
WILEY
2007
BICENTENNIAL

Wiley Publishing, Inc.

Published by Wiley Publishing, Inc., Hoboken, New Jersey
Published simultaneously in Canada

The publisher and the author make no representations or warranties with respect to the accuracy or completeness of the contents of this work and specifically disclaim all warranties, including without limitation warranties of fitness for a particular purpose. No warranty may be created or extended by sales or promotional materials. The advice and strategies contained herein may not be suitable for every situation. This work is sold with the understanding that the publisher is not engaged in rendering legal, accounting, or other professional services. If professional assistance is required, the services of a competent professional person should be sought. Neither the publisher nor the author shall be liable for damages arising here from. The fact that an organization or Website is referred to in this work as a citation and/or a potential source of further information does not mean that the author or the publisher endorses the information the organization or Website may provide or recommendations it may make. Further, readers should be aware that Internet Websites listed in this work may have changed or disappeared between when this work was written and when it is read.

Trademarks: Wiley, the Wiley Publishing logo, and related trademarks are trademarks or registered trademarks of John Wiley & Sons, Inc. and/or its affiliates. SAT is a registered trademark of The College Board. ACT is a registered trademark of ACT, Inc. GRE is a registered trademark of Educational Testing Services. LSAT is a registered trademark of Law School Admission Council. GED is a registered trademark of American Council on Education. GMAT is a registered trademark of Graduate Management Admission Council. All other trademarks are the property of their respective owners. Wiley Publishing, Inc. is not associated with any product or vendor mentioned in this book.

For general information on our other products and services or to obtain technical support please contact our Customer Care Department within the U.S. at (800) 762-2974, outside the U.S. at (317) 572-3993 or fax (317) 572-4002.

Wiley also publishes its books in a variety of electronic formats. Some content that appears in print may not be available in electronic books. For more information about Wiley products, please visit our web site at www.wiley.com.

Library of Congress Cataloging-in-Publication Data:
Molloy, John T.
  Vocabulary puzzles : the fun way to ace standardized tests / John T. Molloy and Rich Norris.
      p. cm.
  Includes bibliographical references and index.
  ISBN-13: 978-0-470-13510-5 (pbk. : alk. paper)
  ISBN-10: 0-470-13510-7 (alk. paper)
  1. Vocabulary tests—Study guides. 2. Word games. 3. Puzzles. I. Norris, Rich, 1946- II. Title.
  PE1449.M525 2007
  428.1'076--dc22
                                          2007020700
Printed in the United States of America
10 9 8 7 6 5 4 3 2 1

Book design by Erin Zeltner
Cover design by José Almaguer

Book production by Wiley Publishing, Inc. Composition Services

To my wife Maureen and my son Robert.

—John T. Molloy

To my late wife Margie.

—Rich Norris

Table of Contents

Crossword Puzzle Solutions   186

PART 2 Overstudying   195

Matching Columns Set 2   195

PART 3 Vocabulary Flashcards   227

After the Test   305

Introduction

You Must Read This Before Starting

Molloy's Vocabulary Training Course is designed to increase the vocabulary you recognize in context and use when you speak or write—skills that will help you score higher on standardized admissions tests and perform better in college, business, and life. The SAT and similar exams emphasize vocabulary and writing because colleges have found that students with poor vocabularies and inadequate writing skills have difficulty handling college-level material and often do not graduate. Standardized tests are used by admissions officers to identify students who are prepared to handle college-level work.

The courses used to prepare students for these standardized tests often end up teaching little more than how to beat the tests. As a result, students do such things as memorize vocabulary words for the test and never use the words again after taking it. Our objective is to give you a more sophisticated, permanent, and useful vocabulary that will help you do well not only on admissions tests but afterwards as well.

When our students read the hints given in an SAT prep test book, took at least a half dozen prep tests on their own, and carefully went over their answers, their scores went up. They improved because they had become familiar with the test format and had developed techniques for answering questions. We also discovered that when our students took standard SAT courses they improved almost twice as much as they did when working on their own. So we strongly recommend taking a prep course or at least practicing for the test using one of the standard books.

Why then should you spend more time taking my course? The reason is simple. Since the majority of students heading for college or graduate school take an appropriate prep course or prepare for the test on their own, you need to do the same just to stay even. However, if you want to give yourself an edge, you have to do more. This book contains the only course I know that gives you that edge.

If you have any doubt that the vocabulary you use when you speak or write affects what people think of you, consider President George W. Bush. I'm sure if you told your parents that you had been admitted to Yale and assured them that after graduating you intended to go to Harvard for your MBA, they would be more than pleased. In fact, they might be tempted to brag about how smart you are. Yet, even though Bush went to Harvard and Yale, every comedian in the country tells jokes about how dumb he is. His problem is not that he is dumb, but he sometimes gives that appearance when he speaks. I'm sure he has a more extensive vocabulary than many of the comedians who make jokes at his expense; however, the words he knows do not come to him automatically when he is speaking. Bush would appear more articulate and knowledgeable if he spent an hour a night for a few months working on exercises similar to the ones in this book. I'm sure it would work for him because I have trained dozens of business executives who had similar problems.

Research and Findings

I originally developed this course while teaching at a private school in Connecticut in the 1960s. The school developed an SAT course at the request of several parents, and I was asked to teach the verbal section. From the beginning, I approached this task as a researcher and questioned everything about different approaches to teaching vocabulary. By varying my methodology and keeping a running record of the results, I found that I was easily able to improve the students' SAT scores, as well as their writing.

Indeed, I succeeded so well that the parents, many of whom were business executives, soon realized that their children were writing better than many of their workers and began sending their adult employees to my classes. Eventually, I had to ban the business people, because they dominated the younger students in the class. To keep the companies happy, I developed for them a text containing the exercises that I hear is still in use. This book is an expanded and updated version of that early text.

After seven years, I was forced to give up the tutoring, despite its success, as I became more heavily engaged in providing research and advice for businesses across the country. But several years ago I returned to the subject at the suggestion of a math teacher who wanted to join forces in opening test preparation schools (though he later dropped the project). By that time I was running a research company with an entire staff of researchers, who were able to greatly expand my original testing.

My teaching experience and the extensive testing by my staff has led to four conclusions:

1. Most students study vocabulary backwards. They are given a word and asked to come up with its meaning or definition. We reversed the process: We give them a definition and ask them to come up with the word, which is the way people normally use vocabulary. When they write or speak, they usually know what they want to say, but their problem is finding the right word or phrase to express their thoughts. We found that the students we trained using our method were more likely to use their newly acquired vocabulary when they spoke or wrote; hence this is the method we use in this book.

2. Studying the word in context so the students saw how the needed word *fit* into a sentence or passage made it more likely that the student would remember and use the word when a similar context arose.

3. The best way to study new vocabulary is to say and write it at the same time.

4. Although most students believe they know a new vocabulary word, they really don't. New vocabulary words become useful only when using them is more a matter of instinct than mental process. *Overstudying*, that is, continuing to study words even after you believe you know them, is the best way to acquire that sort of instinctual knowledge.

At first I based my conclusions on my experience as a teacher. When students studied by going from definition to word, I saw vocabulary words we taught in class slipping into their compositions, book reports, and essays. The students who studied the same vocabulary by memorizing definitions seldom incorporated the same words into their writing. There were so many variables, however, that I was uncomfortable referring to my teaching results as research and decided it was necessary to conduct an additional study.

After three years of study it became clear that the four conclusions mentioned above were valid. Working this time with a sophisticated research team I made several additional discoveries, not the least of which was how to best present our information in written form. The most difficult thing to ascertain was how often students had to say or write a word before they used it without effort in their writing or speech. I gave several groups of students the same list of words to study. Each group was given slightly different instructions. While one class was instructed to say and then write the words three times, other groups were told to follow the same procedure four times, five times and so forth. Ninety days after they finished studying the list, they were tested. As a result, we concluded that most students had to repeat aloud and write a new vocabulary word from six to twelve times before they *owned* it. The format of this text is based on that study.

While researching the effectiveness of these exercises we made some additional discoveries: The first was that the majority of the students who completed the exercises not only scored higher on the SAT, but also improved their grade-point average both in high school and college. Apparently, teachers grade students not only on what they have learned about a subject, but also how well they express it.

We also discovered that there are two reasons that a student might not use his or her new vocabulary effectively, even after working conscientiously with these exercises. The first reason is that some students are poor spellers and often substitute a less effective word they could spell for one they could not. If you are a poor speller you must make a list of new vocabulary words that you are not sure how to spell and work at learning to spell them. Once you are sure of how to spell them, you will immediately start using a larger percentage of your new vocabulary.

The second reason that some of our students did not use the words they just learned was because many words did not sound right to them. This was a common problem for students for whom English was a second language and those whose families and friends did not use standard English. We also ran across a number of students from upper-middle-class backgrounds who had the same problem. Fortunately, it's easy to overcome.

If a new vocabulary word does not sound right to you, write it in three sentences and read those sentences aloud half a dozen times a day for a week. If the word still sounds strange, repeat the exercises until it sounds fine. Don't worry. Sooner or later even the strangest-sounding vocabulary words will sound right, if you repeat them aloud in context often enough.

Finally, we concluded that these exercises improved the performance of all students; both those who have been reading challenging material for years and those who hardly ever read an assignment in high school benefited from the experience. It works for anyone who puts in the time and effort to repeatedly use newly acquired vocabulary in context. Every exercise in this book is designed to help you do just that.

How This Book's Organization and Exercises Help You

This book is divided into three sections, each with exercises scientifically designed to give you a larger, more sophisticated, useful, and permanent vocabulary. In Part 1 you not only complete crossword puzzles made up of potential test words, but you also use new vocabulary words in context. In addition, you are instructed to use each word in two sentences and to write unfamiliar vocabulary words three times. Why put so much time and effort into studying words you are convinced you already know? We found that newly acquired vocabulary words effortlessly slip into students' writing if they use them in context a minimum of a half-dozen times after they think they know them. That is why Part 2 requires that you double your efforts to study words you are convinced you already know. If you don't do the exercises in Part 2, you should at least recognize most of the new words you studied when you run across them while reading. However, when writing an essay under the pressure of a timed exam—as students are expected to do on standardized tests— most students use only a small percentage of their new vocabulary and rely almost entirely on their instinctive vocabulary. Years of testing and teaching vocabulary for these standardized tests has convinced us that the best way to make a newly acquired vocabulary word instinctive is to use it over and over in context. That is exactly what the exercises in Part 2 force you to do.

Students who complete Part 2 within 90 days of taking the SAT or similar test are most likely to incorporate their new vocabulary into their writing. Keep in mind this 90-day advantage. If you can arrange to do or review Part 2 just before taking the test, do so; it will help. You also can use the flashcards in Part 3 for this review.

This course is a product of testing and that is why you must follow the instructions in this book exactly. Doing so will give you an edge on standardized tests—in college, in graduate school, and in life.

So, let's get started!

John T. Molloy

Learning Definitions and Using Words in Context

The clues in these puzzles include definitions of some of our new vocabulary words. If you know or can figure out the definition from the puzzle itself, that's great. If not, you can look up the definition and a sample sentence in the flash-cards in Part 3 of this book.

Clues appearing in solid capital letters are definitions of new vocabulary words. You may already know some of these words or be able to figure them out by working with the puzzle. But don't be surprised if some of these words are harder for you than other words in the puzzle. When a clue word has an asterisk, then the word in the clue is on the vocabulary list.

Puzzle 1

Step 1: Crossword Puzzle

Work on this crossword for no more than 15 minutes. If an answer does not occur to you after you've given it some thought, move on. It is possible that you will not complete the puzzle in the allotted time; it is not important that you do. What is important is that you work at it conscientiously for the full 15 minutes.

Across

1. Disease-fighting fluid
3. Give implied approval to; overlook (something illegal)
8. Abbreviation meaning "Just in case you wanted to know"
9. Lethal*; deadly
12. FAVORING POLITICAL REFORM
14. EASILY SEEN OR NOTICED
17. Estimable* baseball pitcher
19. MADE UP OF SELECTIONS FROM VARIOUS SOURCES
22. Eccentric* person
23. What @ means, in URLs
24. Numbered book parts
25. MEDICAL REHABILITATION PROCESS
28. Quick ___ wink: 2 wds.
30. Cyclical* ocean movement
32. Competed in a marathon
33. AGREEMENT; MUSICAL PART THAT BLENDS WITH THE MELODY
34. Do a newspaper job
35. Lose your sunburn

Down

1. ADEQUATE FOR THE PURPOSE; ENOUGH
2. REASONABLE; SENSIBLE
4. TV's *The King* ___ *Queens*
5. Where the Empire State Bldg. is: Abbr.
6. DREADFUL; TERRIBLE
7. Nothing, in Spanish
10. Quantum* ___
11. CHEERFUL WILLINGNESS; EAGERNESS
13. Novel or text
15. CHEERFULLY OPTIMISTIC
16. Puts money (on)
18. Intimation*; hint to an actor
20. DEVIATING FROM THE PROPER COURSE
21. Faucet
26. Adamantine*; not easy
27. Actor Morales
29. Joan of ___
30. Pinnacle*; peak
31. Hair coloring stuff

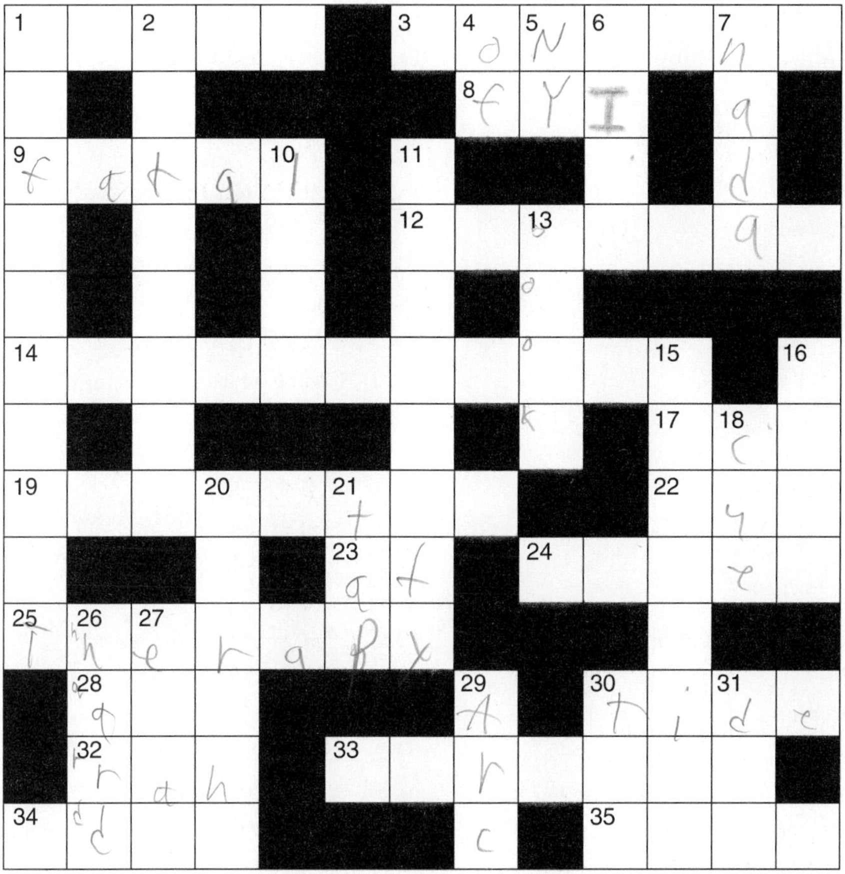

Step 2: Matching Columns

Work as long as necessary on these matching columns. Try to match every word with its definition. If you read carefully the sentences in which the words appear, you will in most cases be able to figure out the meaning of the words. Work diligently at figuring them out; it is a wonderful way to learn vocabulary. If there are words you cannot match, use the flashcards at the back of the book to complete this section. When you have finished, read through the matching columns four times. Each time you read the definition try to use the word in a new sentence. Slow down when you come to the word you're studying and write it. In this exercise, there's no need to write out the entire sentence or even the phrase in which it appears, unless you think that would help you remember the word.

DEFINITION	SAMPLE SENTENCE
_____ dreadful; terrible	A.) The phases of the moon follow a CYCLICAL path.
_____ deviating from the proper course	B.) We must never CONDONE the taking of hostages, no matter what reason.
_____ too hard to cut, break, or pierce	C.) Her CD collection was quite ECLECTIC, as it contained music from hip-hop to Celine Dion.
_____ easily seen or noticed	D.) The old man's ECCENTRIC behavior made him an outcast in his town.
_____ worthy of esteem; excellent	E.) Without the right tools, he could not cut through the ADAMANTINE rock.
_____ give implied approval to; overlook	F.) The outfielder's ERRANT throw went well over the catcher's head.
_____ occurring at regular intervals	G.) When the tornado destroyed their house they were truly in a DIRE situation.
_____ cheerful willingness; eagerness	H.) Barry Bonds has been an ESTIMABLE power hitter in the world of baseball.
_____ made up of selections from various sources	I.) Wearing a Halloween costume on Valentine's Day would make you CONSPICUOUS.
_____ person with a peculiar personality; screwball, nut	J.) She couldn't afford to buy a ticket, so she accepted the invitation to the concert with ALACRITY.

DEFINITION	SAMPLE SENTENCE
_____ adequate for the purpose; enough	A.) The LIBERAL believed no one should be discriminated against because of race or sexual orientation.
_____ hint; cue	B.) When the company doubled the size of the factory, it achieved a QUANTUM increase in production.
_____ sudden and significant	C.) To assure himself as much money as possible, the professional athlete planned to sign a long-term contract at the PINNACLE of his career.
_____ reasonable, sensible	D.) To get rid of his lisp, the school counselor suggested speech THERAPY.
_____ fatal, deadly	E.) His patience and ability to consider all the angles helped him make RATIONAL decisions.
_____ agreement; musical part that blends with the melody	F.) Because she was a straight-A student, she had SANGUINE expectations about being accepted by a good college.
_____ cheerfully optimistic	G.) In the duet, Sharon sang melody, while her partner Felicia sang HARMONY.
_____ favoring political reform	H.) The surprise party was such a well kept secret that she had no INTIMATION of what was about to Happen.
_____ peak; top	I.) With barely $5 in her pocket, she barely had SUFFICIENT money to buy lunch.
_____ medical rehabilitation process	J.) A gun is a LETHAL weapon.

Step 3: Write Sentences

For each word write two sentences that indicate you know the meaning of the word. Then read aloud quickly three times each set of sentences that came to you. If you hesitated before coming up with the sentences or had to look up a word, say each of those sentences six times and write the vocabulary word you are studying at least three times. You can write them anywhere—on the lines after the sentences, in the margin, or on a piece of paper—as long as you write them.

Word: **ADAMANTINE**

Sentence 1:

_____

_____

Sentence 2:

_____

_____

Word: **ALACRITY**

Sentence 1:

_____

_____

Sentence 2:

_____

_____

Word: CONDONE

Sentence 1:

_____

_____

Sentence 2:

_____

_____

Word: CONSPICUOUS

Sentence 1:

_____

_____

Sentence 2:

_____

_____

Word: CYCLICAL

Sentence 1:

_____

_____

Sentence 2:

_____

_____

Word: **DIRE**

Sentence 1:

_____

_____

Sentence 2:

_____

_____

Word: **ECCENTRIC**

Sentence 1:

_____

_____

Sentence 2:

_____

_____

Word: **ECLECTIC**

Sentence 1:

_____

_____

Sentence 2:

_____

_____

Word: **ERRANT**

Sentence 1:

_____

_____

Sentence 2:

_____

_____

Word: **ESTIMABLE**

Sentence 1:

_____

_____

Sentence 2:

_____

_____

Word: **HARMONY**

Sentence 1:

_____

_____

Sentence 2:

_____

_____

Word: INTIMATION

Sentence 1:

_____

_____

Sentence 2:

_____

_____

Word: LETHAL

Sentence 1:

_____

_____

Sentence 2:

_____

_____

Word: LIBERAL (n.)

Sentence 1:

_____

_____

Sentence 2:

_____

_____

Word: **PINNACLE**

Sentence 1:

_____

_____

Sentence 2:

_____

_____

Word: **QUANTUM**

Sentence 1:

_____

_____

Sentence 2:

_____

_____

Word: **RATIONAL**

Sentence 1:

_____

_____

Sentence 2:

_____

_____

Word: SANGUINE

Sentence 1:

_____

_____

Sentence 2:

_____

_____

Word: SUFFICIENT

Sentence 1:

_____

_____

Sentence 2:

_____

_____

Word: THERAPY

Sentence 1:

_____

_____

Sentence 2:

_____

_____

If necessary, return and complete the crossword puzzle in Step I.

Puzzle 2

Step 1: Crossword Puzzle

Work on this crossword for no more than 15 minutes. If an answer does not occur to you after you've given it some thought, move on. It is possible that you will not complete the puzzle in the allotted time; it is not important that you do. What is important is that you work at it conscientiously for the full 15 minutes.

Across

2. MOTIVATED PURELY BY MONEY
8. Response to being famished*
10. Top Olympics medal
11. Despondent*
12. REMOVE FROM POWER
14. Courtroom event
15. DESTINY; FATE
18. What @ means, in Web addresses
20. Lubricate*
21. Hiatus*
22. Eschew*
24. FEELING OF EMBARRASSMENT OR SHAME
26. Wrestler's cushion
27. EXCLUDE; BANISH
29. "___ apple a day..."
30. Negative vote
31. RESPECT OR REVERENCE GIVEN, AS TO A HERO

Down

1. DESOLATE; GRIM; HARSH
3. RESTRICTED TO A PARTICULAR AREA
4. Feeling of self-worth
5. LONGING OR SENTIMENTAL FEELINGS FOR THE PAST
6. Vigilant*
7. Thoroughfare: Abbr.
8. Easy ___ pie
9. Actor Asner or Harris
13. DISRESPECTFUL; IRREVERENT
16. COMPLETE FREEDOM FROM PUNISHMENT
17. Mixer with gin
19. STRONGHOLD; PLACE OF GREAT FORTIFICATION
21. RELEVANT; PERTINENT
23. Entreat*
25. Actor Holm of *The Fellowship of the Ring*
28. Buckle*

Step 2: Matching Columns

Work as long as necessary on these matching columns. Try to match every word with its definition. If you read carefully the sentences in which the words appear, you will in most cases be able to figure out the meaning of the words. Work diligently at figuring them out; it is a wonderful way to learn vocabulary. If there are words you cannot match, use the flashcards at the back of the book to complete this section. When you have finished, read through the matching columns four times. Each time you read the definition try to use the word in a new sentence. Slow down when you come to the word you're studying and write it. In this exercise, there's no need to write out the entire sentence or even the phrase in which it appears, unless you think that would help you remember the word.

DEFINITION	SAMPLE SENTENCE
_____ feeling of embarrassment or shame	A.) The unhappy citizens wanted to DEPOSE the queen.
_____ restricted to a particular area	B.) Her doctor told her to ESCHEW fatty foods.
_____ very hungry	C.) He suffered CHAGRIN when he realized he'd forgotten his friend's birthday.
_____ stronghold; place of fortification	D.) He felt DESPONDENT after losing the big game.
_____ remove from power	E.) America is considered a great BASTION of freedom around the world.
_____ give up one's position, office, or power	F.) The disruptive student made FLIPPANT remarks to the teacher.
_____ sag or collapse under pressure	G.) After not eating all day, he was FAMISHED at dinnertime.
_____ pray; beg	H.) The bridge BUCKLEd because there were too many trucks on it.
_____ disrespectful; irreverent	I.) The angry citizens forced the king to ABDICATE the throne.
_____ feeling hopeless, dejected, or very sad	J.) He ENTREATed the judge for mercy.
_____ keep away from; shun	K.) Only found in Antarctica, the Adélie penguin is ENDEMIC to that region.

DEFINITION	SAMPLE SENTENCE
_____ respect or reverence given, as to a hero	A.) In a debate, keep your answers GERMANE to the subject; don't bring up unrelated issues.
_____ put oil on	B.) When he continued to break the rules at the private club, he was finally OSTRACIZEd from it.
_____ relevant; pertinent	C.) The icy mountain was a STARK land-scape for the climber.
_____ complete freedom from punishment	D.) Heather LUBRICATEd the door to stop it from squeaking.
_____ exclude; banish	E.) When the rioters realized there was a shortage of police, they looted stores with IMPUNITY.
_____ gap	F.) Night watchmen must learn to be VIGILANT no matter how tired they feel.
_____ desolate; grim; harsh	G.) The workers' strike at the factory led to a HIATUS in the work flow.
_____ ever awake and alert	H.) She would not do anything for free; her motives were entirely MERCENARY.
_____ longing or sentimental feelings for the past	I.) My girl thinks we met because of KISMET; I think it was just coinci-dence.
_____ destiny; fate	J.) Listening to the old records evoked a feeling of NOSTALGIA in him.
_____ motivated purely by money	K.) The city paid HOMAGE to the return-ing soldiers in the parade.

Step 3: Write Sentences

For each word write two sentences that indicate you know the meaning of the word. Then read aloud quickly three times each set of sentences that came to you. If you hesitated before coming up with the sentences or had to look up a word, say each of those sentences six times and write the vocabulary word you are studying at least three times. You can write them anywhere—on the lines after the sentences, in the margin, or on a piece of paper—as long as you write them.

Word: **ABDICATE**

Sentence 1:

_____

_____

Sentence 2:

_____

_____

Word: **BUCKLE**

Sentence 1:

_____

_____

Sentence 2:

_____

_____

Word: CHAGRIN

Sentence 1:

_____

_____

Sentence 2:

_____

_____

Word: DEPOSE

Sentence 1:

_____

_____

Sentence 2:

_____

_____

Word: DESPONDENT

Sentence 1:

_____

_____

Sentence 2:

_____

_____

Word: ENDEMIC

Sentence 1:

_____

_____

Sentence 2:

_____

_____

Word: ENTREAT

Sentence 1:

_____

_____

Sentence 2:

_____

_____

Word: ESCHEW

Sentence 1:

_____

_____

Sentence 2:

_____

_____

Word: FAMISHED

Sentence 1:

_____

_____

Sentence 2:

_____

_____

Word: FLIPPANT

Sentence 1:

_____

_____

Sentence 2:

_____

_____

Word: GERMANE

Sentence 1:

_____

_____

Sentence 2:

_____

_____

Word: HIATUS

Sentence 1:

_____

_____

Sentence 2:

_____

_____

Word: HOMAGE

Sentence 1:

_____

_____

Sentence 2:

_____

_____

Word: IMPUNITY

Sentence 1:

_____

_____

Sentence 2:

_____

_____

Word: KISMET

Sentence 1:

_____

_____

Sentence 2:

_____

_____

Word: LUBRICATE

Sentence 1:

_____

_____

Sentence 2:

_____

_____

Word: MERCENARY

Sentence 1:

_____

_____

Sentence 2:

_____

_____

Word: NOSTALGIA

Sentence 1:

_____

_____

Sentence 2:

_____

_____

Word: OSTRACIZE

Sentence 1:

_____

_____

Sentence 2:

_____

_____

Word: STARK

Sentence 1:

_____

_____

Sentence 2:

_____

_____

Word: **VIGILANT**

Sentence 1:

_____

_____

Sentence 2:

_____

_____

If necessary, return and complete the crossword puzzle in Step I.

Puzzle 3

Step 1: Crossword Puzzle

Work on this crossword for no more than 15 minutes. If an answer does not occur to you after you've given it some thought, move on. It is possible that you will not complete the puzzle in the allotted time; it is not important that you do. What is important is that you work at it conscientiously for the full 15 minutes.

Across

1. SEPARATIONS IN A GROUP, ESPECIALLY DUE TO A DISAGREEMENT
5. Gratuity*
6. Arbiter* in boxing matches
9. Majestic* mountain in Europe
11. Blunder*
14. GRUESOME; HORRIBLE
15. STRONGLY AFFECTING ONE'S EMOTIONS
16. Wedding promise: 2 words
18. Only one of the Seven Dwarfs who wears spectacles
20. SHOWING GREAT INTENSITY OF SPIRIT; PASSIONATE; HEATED
21. Stomach muscles, for short
23. DECEIVE; TRICK
25. Exist
26. Grandiloquent* speaker
29. Roman emperor with a fiddle
30. PLEASANT MEANS OF AMUSEMENT OR RECREATION
32. LESSEN; REDUCE

Down

1. NOT GENUINE OR AUTHENTIC; COUNTERFEIT
2. Abbreviation before a man's name
3. Symbol of authenticity*
4. INCLINED TO SEEK REVENGE
5. TREMBLING FEAR
7. Winter ailment
8. UNEXPECTED GAIN OR GOOD FORTUNE
10. WISE IN PRACTICAL MATTERS; SENSIBLE
12. Fishing need
13. DISPARAGING* HINT OR IMPLICATION ABOUT SOMEONE OR SOMETHING
17. SHAKE OR WAVE, AS A WEAPON
19. "___ your mark, get set, go!"
22. World War I spy Mata ___
24. TV medical show
25. Protuberance* in the road
27. Stop sign color
28. Actor Selleck
30. Greek letter used in algebra
31. Shakespeare's ___ *You Like It*

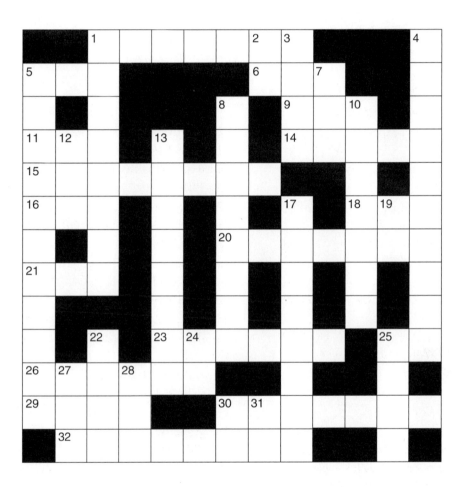

Step 2: Matching Columns

Work as long as necessary on these matching columns. Try to match every word with its definition. If you read carefully the sentences in which the words appear, you will in most cases be able to figure out the meaning of the words. Work diligently at figuring them out; it is a wonderful way to learn vocabulary. If there are words you cannot match, use the flashcards at the back of the book to complete this section. When you have finished, read through the matching columns four times. Each time you read the definition try to use the word in a new sentence. Slow down when you come to the word you're studying and write it. In this exercise, there's no need to write out the entire sentence or even the phrase in which it appears, unless you think that would help you remember the word.

DEFINITION	SAMPLE SENTENCE
_____ to make a mistake; err	A.) The planner BLUNDERed when he scheduled two games on the same field at the same time.
_____ speaking in a lofty style, as an orator	B.) Shakespeare's villain Iago DELUDEd Othello into thinking he was his friend.
_____ person with power to decide; judge; referee	C.) Her disappointing SAT scores DIMINISHed her chances of getting into the college of her choice.
_____ unfairly characterizing as unimportant	D.) The home plate umpire is the ARBITER of balls and strikes.
_____ deceive; trick	E.) Unable to find any information that might damage his opponent, the politician resorted to insults and INNUENDOes.
_____ shake or wave, as a weapon	F.) The recommended GRATUITY when dining out is 15 percent of the bill.
_____ tip to a waiter	G.) He BRANDISHed the knife to frighten his attacker.
_____ lessen; reduce	H.) The cheerleaders were FERVENT in their show of support for the team.
_____ the quality of being genuine	I.) The candidates spoke GRANDILOQUENTly in the debate.
_____ disparaging hint or implication about someone or something	J.) In the nasty political race, the two candidates made DISPARAGING remarks about each other's abilities.
_____ showing great intensity of spirit; passionate; heated	K.) The Great Seal of the United States assures the AUTHENTICITY of paper money.

DEFINITION	SAMPLE SENTENCE
_____ separation in a group, especially due to disagreement	A.) When oil prices went up sharply due to a shortage, oil companies experienced a WINDFALL.
_____ pleasant means of amusement or recreation	B.) Reports of UFOs over the town turned out to be SPURIOUS.
_____ inclined to seek revenge	C.) When the lovers parted at the end of the film, it was a POIGNANT moment for the entire audience.
_____ gruesome; horrible	D.) A SCHISM has formed in some religious organizations over gay rights.
_____ part that sticks out; bulge; bump	E.) Alone in the house, he felt TREPIDATION when the wind made the roof creak.
_____ of lofty dignity or imposing aspect	F.) It is PRUDENT not to walk in certain neighborhoods after dark.
_____ unexpected gain or good fortune	G.) The mountains were a MAJESTIC sight when viewed from the nearby desert.
_____ strongly affecting one's emotions	H.) Baseball is our country's national PASTIME.
_____ trembling fear	I.) The tree trunk had a PROTUBERANCE where a branch had been mostly cut off.
_____ not genuine or authentic; counterfeit	J.) The *Scream* film series contained many LURID scenes.
_____ wise in practical matters; sensible	K.) It is usually better to understand and forgive someone who hurts you, rather than be VINDICTIVE.

Step 3: Write Sentences

For each word write two sentences that indicate you know the meaning of the word. Then read aloud quickly three times each set of sentences that came to you. If you hesitated before coming up with the sentences or had to look up a word, say each of those sentences six times and write the vocabulary word you are studying at least three times. You can write them anywhere—on the lines after the sentences, in the margin, or on a piece of paper—as long as you write them.

Word: **ARBITER**

Sentence 1:

_____

_____

Sentence 2:

_____

_____

Word: **AUTHENTICITY**

Sentence 1:

_____

_____

Sentence 2:

_____

_____

Word: **BLUNDER**

Sentence 1:

_____

_____

Sentence 2:

_____

_____

Word: **BRANDISH**

Sentence 1:

_____

_____

Sentence 2:

_____

_____

Word: **DELUDE**

Sentence 1:

_____

_____

Sentence 2:

_____

_____

Word: DIMINISH

Sentence 1:

_____

_____

Sentence 2:

_____

_____

Word: DISPARAGING

Sentence 1:

_____

_____

Sentence 2:

_____

_____

Word: FERVENT

Sentence 1:

_____

_____

Sentence 2:

_____

_____

Word: **GRANDILOQUENT**

Sentence 1:

_____

_____

Sentence 2:

_____

_____

Word: **GRATUITY**

Sentence 1:

_____

_____

Sentence 2:

_____

_____

Word: **INNUENDO**

Sentence 1:

_____

_____

Sentence 2:

_____

_____

Word: LURID

Sentence 1:

_____

_____

Sentence 2:

_____

_____

Word: MAJESTIC

Sentence 1:

_____

_____

Sentence 2:

_____

_____

Word: PASTIME

Sentence 1:

_____

_____

Sentence 2:

_____

_____

Word: POIGNANT

Sentence 1:

_____

_____

Sentence 2:

_____

_____

Word: PROTUBERANCE

Sentence 1:

_____

_____

Sentence 2:

_____

_____

Word: PRUDENT

Sentence 1:

_____

_____

Sentence 2:

_____

_____

Word: **SCHISM**

Sentence 1:

_____

_____

Sentence 2:

_____

_____

Word: **SPURIOUS**

Sentence 1:

_____

_____

Sentence 2:

_____

_____

Word: **TREPIDATION**

Sentence 1:

_____

_____

Sentence 2:

_____

_____

Word: **VINDICTIVE**

Sentence 1:

_____

_____

Sentence 2:

_____

_____

Word: **WINDFALL**

Sentence 1:

_____

_____

Sentence 2:

_____

_____

If necessary, return and complete the crossword puzzle in Step I.

Puzzle 4

Step 1: Crossword Puzzle

Work on this crossword for no more than 15 minutes. If an answer does not occur to you after you've given it some thought, move on. It is possible that you will not complete the puzzle in the allotted time; it is not important that you do. What is important is that you work at it conscientiously for the full 15 minutes.

Across

2. BOLD IN A RUDE WAY
6. Garbage boat
9. Bird that's a peace symbol
10. ARROGANT PRIDE
12. Ornamental* vase
13. "So long!"
16. GIVEN TO PLAYFUL HUMOR
19. Toy in a model house
20. DISRESPECTFUL IN A BOLD WAY
23. Trig or calc
25. CLEVER VERBAL EXCHANGE; WITTY REMARKS
27. Breakfast drink, as it's familiarly called
28. TALK DOWN TO; TREAT AS IN INFERIOR
29. TV show with trauma* cases
30. Apathetic*; showing little or no emotion

Down

1. "Person, place, or thing" part of speech
3. ACT OF GOING WITHOUT SOMETHING
4. Expunges* from the text, for example
5. Negative answer
7. OCCURRING REGULARLY OVER A LONG PERIOD
8. The ___ (*Smallville* network)
11. INCLINED TO BELIEVE ANYTHING; NAIVE
14. Opposite of P.M.
15. Succor*
17. SECRET; UNDERCOVER
18. Former vice president Gore
21. LONG, ANGRY SPEECH
22. AVOID A RESPONSIBILITY
23. Act dejectedly*
24. Open a minuscule* amount, as a door
25. Littlest of the litter
26. Nefarious*; wicked

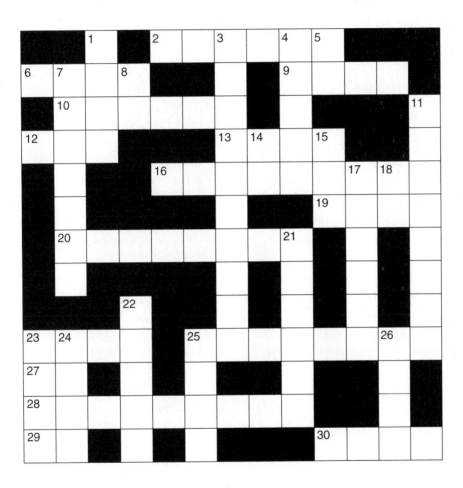

Step 2: Matching Columns

Work as long as necessary on these matching columns. Try to match every word with its definition. If you read carefully the sentences in which the words appear, you will in most cases be able to figure out the meaning of the words. Work diligently at figuring them out; it is a wonderful way to learn vocabulary. If there are words you cannot match, use the flashcards at the back of the book to complete this section. When you have finished, read through the matching columns four times. Each time you read the definition try to use the word in a new sentence. Slow down when you come to the word you're studying and write it. In this exercise, there's no need to write out the entire sentence or even the phrase in which it appears, unless you think that would help you remember the word.

DEFINITION	SAMPLE SENTENCE
_____ inclined to believe anything; naïve	A.) She developed CHRONIC sneezing during the allergy season.
_____ secret; undercover	B.) Because of his HUBRIS, he truly expected to be voted the best-looking guy in the school.
_____ disrespectful in a bold way	C.) George was trying to lose weight, so he practiced ABSTINENCE when it came to eating fatty foods.
_____ the act of going without something	D.) The spy was assigned to a COVERT operation.
_____ arrogant pride	E.) The IMPUDENT child publicly was rude to his father.
_____ bold in a rude way	F.) Young children are GULLIBLE and easy to fool.
_____ erase or strike out	G.) He never said he was DEJECTED, but we could tell from the way he moped all the time.
_____ unhappy; miserable	H.) Surprisingly, Joanne seemed APATHETIC when told her mother was seriously ill.
_____ occurring regularly over a long period	I.) The editor EXPUNGEd the unnecessary paragraph from the story.
_____ showing little or no emotion; cold	J.) The class was shocked at the BRAZEN remarks the student made to the teacher.

DEFINITION	SAMPLE SENTENCE
_____ long, angry speech	A.) My boss never treated the workers as equals; he seemed to enjoy PATRONIZing them instead.
_____ clear verbal exchange; witty remarks	B.) Since it was cold out, he opened the window a MINUSCULE amount to let in some air.
_____ given to playful humor	C.) He was brought to the emergency room suffering severe TRAUMA from the auto accident.
_____ avoid a responsibility	D.) The FBI tried to thwart his NEFARIOUS plan to blow up the building.
_____ tiny	E.) If you SHIRK your homework, you won't get good grades.
_____ shock from a serious injury	F.) The comedian came out on top in his REPARTEE with the heckler.
_____ talk down to; treat as an inferior	G.) Instead of discussing his own ideas, the politician launched into a TIRADE about his opponent's platform.
_____ help; aid	H.) We hang ORNAMENTAL lights on our Christmas tree each year.
_____ decorative	I.) The community required SUCCOR from the government after the tornado hit.
_____ extremely wicked or villainous	J.) Though her political cartoons were focused on the issues, they were often WHIMSICAL as well.

Step 3: Write Sentences

For each word write two sentences that indicate you know the meaning of the word. Then read aloud quickly three times each set of sentences that came to you. If you hesitated before coming up with the sentences or had to look up a word, say each of those sentences six times and write the vocabulary word you are studying at least three times. You can write them anywhere—on the lines after the sentences, in the margin, or on a piece of paper—as long as you write them.

Word: ABSTINENCE

Sentence 1:

_____

_____

Sentence 2:

_____

_____

Word: APATHETIC

Sentence 1:

_____

_____

Sentence 2:

_____

_____

Word: BRAZEN

Sentence 1:

_____

_____

Sentence 2:

_____

_____

Word: CHRONIC

Sentence 1:

_____

_____

Sentence 2:

_____

_____

Word: COVERT

Sentence 1:

_____

_____

Sentence 2:

_____

_____

Word: DEJECTED

Sentence 1:

_____

_____

Sentence 2:

_____

_____

Word: EXPUNGE

Sentence 1:

_____

_____

Sentence 2:

_____

_____

Word: GULLIBLE

Sentence 1:

_____

_____

Sentence 2:

_____

_____

Word: HUBRIS

Sentence 1:

_____

_____

Sentence 2:

_____

_____

Word: IMPUDENT

Sentence 1:

_____

_____

Sentence 2:

_____

_____

Word: MINUSCULE

Sentence 1:

_____

_____

Sentence 2:

_____

_____

Word: NEFARIOUS

Sentence 1:

_____

_____

Sentence 2:

_____

_____

Word: ORNAMENTAL

Sentence 1:

_____

_____

Sentence 2:

_____

_____

Word: PATRONIZE

Sentence 1:

_____

_____

Sentence 2:

_____

_____

Word: REPARTEE

Sentence 1:

_____

_____

Sentence 2:

_____

_____

Word: SHIRK

Sentence 1:

_____

_____

Sentence 2:

_____

_____

Word: SUCCOR

Sentence 1:

_____

_____

Sentence 2:

_____

_____

Word: TIRADE

Sentence 1:

_____

_____

Sentence 2:

_____

_____

Word: TRAUMA

Sentence 1:

_____

_____

Sentence 2:

_____

_____

Word: WHIMSICAL

Sentence 1:

_____

_____

Sentence 2:

_____

_____

If necessary, return and complete the crossword puzzle in Step I.

Puzzle 5

Step 1: Crossword Puzzle

Work on this crossword for no more than 15 minutes. If an answer does not occur to you after you've given it some thought, move on. It is possible that you will not complete the puzzle in the allotted time; it is not important that you do. What is important is that you work at it conscientiously for the full 15 minutes.

Across

3. Adroitly* escapes from
7. PEACEFUL; CHARMINGLY SIMPLE
9. Monopolize*; take more than your fair share
11. Snow remover
13. CURE-ALL
14. "Phone home" movie alien
15. Burglarize*
17. UNDERSTOOD BY ONLY A FEW
19. Continent where 13-Down is: Abbr.
20. Hartford is its capital: Abbr.
21. IMAGE, SOMETIMES A SACRED* ONE
23. RETREAT TO AN EARLIER STAGE; PROGRESS BACKWARDS
24. FORGO; AVOID
26. List of choices, as on a computer
27. "Are you a man ___ a mouse?"
28. Time between lunch and evening: Abbr.
29. SOOTHE OR RELIEVE

Down

1. TENDING TO BELITTLE OR FIND FAULT WITH
2. Archaic*
4. SOMETHING PASSED DOWN TO FOLLOWING GENERATIONS
5. SHOW DISRESPECT FOR SOMETHING HOLY OR SACRED
6. Diffident*
8. Kind of room on the Web
10. Light switch position
12. WILD AND RECKLESS
13. Country of the Incas
16. BLUNT OR ROUGH IN MANNER
18. HAVING A DREAMLIKE QUALITY
19. "Get lost!"
22. OPEN TO VIEW; NOT SECRET
25. It follows a dot in many addresses
27. *The Wizard* ___ *Oz*

Step 2: Matching Columns

Work as long as necessary on these matching columns. Try to match every word with its definition. If you read carefully the sentences in which the words appear, you will in most cases be able to figure out the meaning of the words. Work diligently at figuring them out; it is a wonderful way to learn vocabulary. If there are words you cannot match, use the flashcards at the back of the book to complete this section. When you have finished, read through the matching columns four times. Each time you read the definition try to use the word in a new sentence. Slow down when you come to the word you're studying and write it. In this exercise, there's no need to write out the entire sentence or even the phrase in which it appears, unless you think that would help you remember the word.

DEFINITION	SAMPLE SENTENCE
_____ blunt or rough in manner	A.) We had to buy a new TV because ours was taken when the house was BURGLARIZEd.
_____ show disrespect for something holy or sacred	B.) If you're on a low-cholesterol diet, you should ESCHEW red meat.
_____ image, sometimes a sacred one	C.) Words like "thou" and "methinks" are considered ARCHAIC nowadays.
_____ tending to belittle or find fault with	D.) After the heist, the robber ADROITly eluded the police for weeks.
_____ clever; skillful	E.) They DESECRATEd the church when they spray-painted graffiti on its walls.
_____ forego; avoid	F.) Advanced techniques of computer programming are quite ABSTRUSE.
_____ rob; steal from	G.) Rather than deal with the issues in the election, she made DISPARAGING remarks about her opponent.
_____ understood by only a few	H.) Many ICONs of saints and angels were on display in the church.
_____ old, from an earlier period	I.) Because he was so DIFFIDENT, he couldn't bring himself to ask her to dance.
_____ shy, timid	J.) The clerk's replies became BRUSQUE when the customer kept repeating the same questions.

DEFINITION	SAMPLE SENTENCE
_____ cure-all	A.) It's not healthy for an adult to REGRESS to childhood by crying and carrying on when he doesn't get what he wants.
_____ take more than your fair share; hog	B.) To Muslims, Mecca is a SACRED place.
_____ peaceful; charmingly simple	C.) When she suffered scrapes in a fall, her mom's tender loving care helped to MOLLIFY her discomfort.
_____ having a dreamlike quality	D.) The New York Yankees' LEGACY of World Series victories may never be surpassed.
_____ soothe or relieve	E.) He enjoyed an IDYLLIC life on the small island.
_____ wild and reckless	F.) Instead of holding it in, she showed OVERT anger by yelling and screaming.
_____ open to view; not secret	G.) The angry mob was responsible for WANTON destruction of store windows.
_____ something passed down to following generations	H.) Whenever she was at a party with Jim, she always MONOPOLIZEd his attention.
_____ retreat to an earlier stage; progress backwards	I.) Many horror movie scenes have an eerie, SURREAL quality about them.
_____ dedicated to some religious purpose; holy	J.) Scientists have yet to find a PANACEA for cancer.

Step 3: Write Sentences

For each word write two sentences that indicate you know the meaning of the word. Then read aloud quickly three times each set of sentences that came to you. If you hesitated before coming up with the sentences or had to look up a word, say each of those sentences six times and write the vocabulary word you are studying at least three times. You can write them anywhere—on the lines after the sentences, in the margin, or on a piece of paper—as long as you write them.

Word: ABSTRUSE

Sentence 1:

_____

_____

Sentence 2:

_____

_____

Word: ADROIT

Sentence 1:

_____

_____

Sentence 2:

_____

_____

Word: ARCHAIC

Sentence 1:

_____

_____

Sentence 2:

_____

_____

Word: BRUSQUE

Sentence 1:

_____

_____

Sentence 2:

_____

_____

Word: BURGLARIZE

Sentence 1:

_____

_____

Sentence 2:

_____

_____

Word: DESECRATE

Sentence 1:

_____

_____

Sentence 2:

_____

_____

Word: DIFFIDENT

Sentence 1:

_____

_____

Sentence 2:

_____

_____

Word: DISPARAGING

Sentence 1:

_____

_____

Sentence 2:

_____

_____

Word: ESCHEW

Sentence 1:

_____

_____

Sentence 2:

_____

_____

Word: ICON

Sentence 1:

_____

_____

Sentence 2:

_____

_____

Word: IDYLLIC

Sentence 1:

_____

_____

Sentence 2:

_____

_____

Word: LEGACY

Sentence 1:

_____

_____

Sentence 2:

_____

_____

Word: MOLLIFY

Sentence 1:

_____

_____

Sentence 2:

_____

_____

Word: MONOPOLIZE

Sentence 1:

_____

_____

Sentence 2:

_____

_____

Word: OVERT

Sentence 1:

_____

_____

Sentence 2:

_____

_____

Word: PANACEA

Sentence 1:

_____

_____

Sentence 2:

_____

_____

Word: REGRESS

Sentence 1:

_____

_____

Sentence 2:

_____

_____

Word: SACRED

Sentence 1:

_____

_____

Sentence 2:

_____

_____

Word: SURREAL

Sentence 1:

_____

_____

Sentence 2:

_____

_____

Word: WANTON

Sentence 1:

_____

_____

Sentence 2:

_____

_____

If necessary, return and complete the crossword puzzle in Step I.

Puzzle 6

Step 1: Crossword Puzzle

Work on this crossword for no more than 15 minutes. If an answer does not occur to you after you've given it some thought, move on. It is possible that you will not complete the puzzle in the allotted time; it is not important that you do. What is important is that you work at it conscientiously for the full 15 minutes.

Across

1. PERSON OF PROFOUND LEARNING; SCHOLAR
6. Shout at the bullfight
7. FREE FROM BLAME
11. Film director Spike
12. Vagrant*; tramp
13. HELP SPEED THINGS ALONG
14. Snapple beverage
16. CENTRAL PART AROUND WHICH OTHER PARTS ARE GATHERED; CORE
18. KIND; GOOD-NATURED DISPOSITION
19. SHARPLY AFFECTING ONE'S SENSE OF TASTE OR SMELL; HOT; PEPPERY
20. OF UNMATCHING PARTS; LACKING HARMONY
23. INAPPROPRIATE LIGHT HUMOR
26. Pecuniary* bills
28. CRUDE; INSENSITIVE

Down

1. SERIOUS AND DIGNIFIED
2. Actor Baldwin or infielder Rodriguez
3. Informal term for a vice president
4. QUIET; NOT INCLINED TO TALK
5. Word from a ghost
8. That lady
9. Pound: Abbr.
10. EXTREMELY HUNGRY; ALMOST IMPOSSIBLE TO SATISFY
14. ACTING TO OVERTHROW ONE'S GOVERNMENT OR RULER, OR HELPING YOUR COUNTRY'S ENEMY
15. HIGHEST POINT
17. DISTRUSTFUL OF THE TRUE MOTIVES OF OTHERS
19. EASY TO BEND; FLEXIBLE
21. SPOKEN WITH CONFIDENCE, BUT NOT MUCH THOUGHT
22. Residue* from burning
24. Ten ___ one odds
25. Greeting from Rocky
26. 101, in old Rome
27. "___ I was saying..."

Step 2: Matching Columns

Work as long as necessary on these matching columns. Try to match every word with its definition. If you read carefully the sentences in which the words appear, you will in most cases be able to figure out the meaning of the words. Work diligently at figuring them out; it is a wonderful way to learn vocabulary. If there are words you cannot match, use the flashcards at the back of the book to complete this section. When you have finished, read through the matching columns four times. Each time you read the definition try to use the word in a new sentence. Slow down when you come to the word you're studying and write it. In this exercise, there's no need to write out the entire sentence or even the phrase in which it appears, unless you think that would help you remember the word.

DEFINITION	SAMPLE SENTENCE
_____ kind; good-natured disposition	A.) Good teamwork by the students EXPEDITEd the completion of their project.
_____ related to money	B.) Some voters were CYNICAL of the shady politician's reasons for holding the fundraising dinner.
_____ spoken with confidence, but not much thought	C.) The king was well-liked because of his BENIGN disposition.
_____ free from blame	D.) Putting the rapper and the folk singer together in the same concert seemed INCONGRUOUS to us.
_____ inappropriate light humor	E.) The candidate's GLIB answers at the press conference cost him a lot of votes.
_____ help speed things along	F.) They couldn't afford to take a trip this year because they were having PECUNIARY trouble.
_____ central part around which other parts are gathered; core	G.) Peter was ABSOLVEd of guilt when John testified that the two of them were together on the night of the robbery.
_____ crude; insensitive	H.) LEVITY at a funeral might not be appreciated by the deceased's family.
_____ of unmatching parts; lacking harmony	I.) He hurt her feelings by making BOORISH remarks about her painting.
_____ distrustful of the motives of others	J.) A small group of friends formed the NUCLEUS of the club.

DEFINITION	SAMPLE SENTENCE
_____ serious and dignified	A.) In the '50s, the Rosenbergs were found guilty of TREASON for selling atom bomb secrets to the Russians.
_____ highest point	B.) John cleaned his shoes after the hike, but there was still a RESIDUE of mud on them.
_____ sharply affecting one's sense of taste or smell; hot; peppery	C.) Our dog has such a VORACIOUS appetite all the time that you'd think we never feed him.
_____ quiet; not inclined to talk	D.) Modelers like to work with clay because it's a PLIANT material.
_____ something that remains; remnant	E.) The city tried to provide shelters for VAGRANTs so they wouldn't have to sleep on the streets.
_____ easy to bend; flexible	F.) At its ZENITH, the company made more computers than anyone else.
_____ extremely hungry; almost impossible to satisfy	G.) He was quite TACITURN at parties, making it difficult to have a conversation with him.
_____ person of profound learning; scholar	H.) The PUNGENT onions made her cry when she was slicing them.
_____ person who wanders about with no employment or home; hobo	I.) Only a SAVANT can truly understand the complexities of nuclear physics.
_____ acting to overthrow one's government or ruler, or helping your country's enemy	J.) The Easter service in honor of Christ was a SOLEMN event.

Step 3: Write Sentences

For each word write two sentences that indicate you know the meaning of the word. Then read aloud quickly three times each set of sentences that came to you. If you hesitated before coming up with the sentences or had to look up a word, say each of those sentences six times and write the vocabulary word you are studying at least three times. You can write them anywhere—on the lines after the sentences, in the margin, or on a piece of paper—as long as you write them.

Word: ABSOLVE

Sentence 1:

_____

_____

Sentence 2:

_____

_____

Word: BENIGN

Sentence 1:

_____

_____

Sentence 2:

_____

_____

Word: BOORISH

Sentence 1:

_____

_____

Sentence 2:

_____

_____

Word: CYNICAL

Sentence 1:

_____

_____

Sentence 2:

_____

_____

Word: EXPEDITE

Sentence 1:

_____

_____

Sentence 2:

_____

_____

Word: GLIB

Sentence 1:

_____

_____

Sentence 2:

_____

_____

Word: INCONGRUOUS

Sentence 1:

_____

_____

Sentence 2:

_____

_____

Word: LEVITY

Sentence 1:

_____

_____

Sentence 2:

_____

_____

Word: NUCLEUS

Sentence 1:

_____

_____

Sentence 2:

_____

_____

Word: PECUNIARY

Sentence 1:

_____

_____

Sentence 2:

_____

_____

Word: PLIANT

Sentence 1:

_____

_____

Sentence 2:

_____

_____

Word: PUNGENT

Sentence 1:

_____

_____

Sentence 2:

_____

_____

Word: RESIDUE

Sentence 1:

_____

_____

Sentence 2:

_____

_____

Word: SAVANT

Sentence 1:

_____

_____

Sentence 2:

_____

_____

Word: SOLEMN

Sentence 1:

_____

_____

Sentence 2:

_____

_____

Word: TACITURN

Sentence 1:

_____

_____

Sentence 2:

_____

_____

Word: TREASON

Sentence 1:

_____

_____

Sentence 2:

_____

_____

Word: VAGRANT

Sentence 1:

_____

_____

Sentence 2:

_____

_____

Word: VORACIOUS

Sentence 1:

_____

_____

Sentence 2:

_____

_____

Word: ZENITH

Sentence 1:

_____

_____

Sentence 2:

_____

_____

If necessary, return and complete the crossword puzzle in Step I.

Puzzle 7

Step 1: Crossword Puzzle

Work on this crossword for no more than 15 minutes. If an answer does not occur to you after you've given it some thought, move on. It is possible that you will not complete the puzzle in the allotted time; it is not important that you do. What is important is that you work at it conscientiously for the full 15 minutes.

Across

1. INTENTIONAL EXAGGERATION
5. It's tasty on chips
7. HAVING A NEGATIVE REPUTATION; FAMOUS FOR SOMETHING BAD
10. SHORTEN OR REDUCE
12. Trapeze artist's safety feature
14. Allow
16. Domesticated* animal
17. ONE PRETENDING TO HAVE KNOWLEDGE HE DOESN'T REALLY HAVE; IMPOSTER
20. Soft fabric used for robes
21. WEALTH AND LUXURY
23. Not at home
25. Baseball player who bats but doesn't field: Abbr.
27. FALSE, THOUGH APPEARING TO BE TRUE
28. Richmond is its capital: Abbr.
29. INACTIVE OR SLUGGISH

Down

1. Sultry*; sweltering
2. SHARP TO THE TASTE
3. Had the deed to
4. MAKE WORSE; AGGRAVATE
5. ODDLY COMICAL
6. NO LONGER FASHIONABLE; OUT-OF-DATE
8. Museum display
9. INCLINED TO PICK FIGHTS; QUARRELSOME
11. "Let It ___" (Beatles song)
13. CATEGORY OR KIND, AS IN AN ART FORM
15. SATIRIZE; PARODY; POKE FUN AT
16. MAKE EXTREMELY DRY OR THIRSTY
18. COMPASSIONATE; SENSITIVE TO OTHERS' FEELINGS
19. SOFTENED; REDUCED IN VOLUME
22. Agenda*
24. Toward the sky
26. Incensed*; angry
28. LX divided by X

Step 2: Matching Columns

Work as long as necessary on these matching columns. Try to match every word with its definition. If you read carefully the sentences in which the words appear, you will in most cases be able to figure out the meaning of the words. Work diligently at figuring them out; it is a wonderful way to learn vocabulary. If there are words you cannot match, use the flashcards at the back of the book to complete this section. When you have finished, read through the matching columns four times. Each time you read the definition try to use the word in a new sentence. Slow down when you come to the word you're studying and write it. In this exercise, there's no need to write out the entire sentence or even the phrase in which it appears, unless you think that would help you remember the word.

DEFINITION	SAMPLE SENTENCE
_____ having a negative reputation; famous for something bad	A.) Stephen King is a master of the horror GENRE.
_____ oddly comical	B.) Lying about why she missed the exam only EXACERBATEd the situation.
_____ intentional exaggeration	C.) The BELLICOSE leader constantly had his country on the brink of war.
_____ inclined to pick fights; quarrelsome	D.) When the doctor continued to make incorrect diagnoses, we knew he was probably a CHARLATAN.
_____ category or kind, as in an art form	E.) The comedian delivered jokes in a DROLL monotone.
_____ angry; mad	F.) "We had to wait an eternity" is an example of HYPERBOLE.
_____ one pretending to have knowledge he doesn't really have; imposter	G.) Dictionaries are often ABRIDGEd to make them smaller and easier to use.
_____ to make worse; aggravate	H.) John's dad became INCENSED when he learned John had gotten a speeding ticket the first night he drove the car.
_____ tame	I.) Bonnie and Clyde were two of the most INFAMOUS criminals in modern history.
_____ shorten or reduce	J.) Tigers aren't DOMESTICATED so they don't make good house pets.

DEFINITION	SAMPLE SENTENCE
_____ make extremely dry or thirsty	A.) He always felt TORPID during the hot summer months.
_____ sharp to the taste	B.) Even though their conversation was MUTED, the librarian asked them to stop talking.
_____ inactive or sluggish	C.) The salsa was so PIQUANT that she thought her tongue would catch fire.
_____ satirize; parody; poke fun at	D.) We endured a string of SULTRY days during the heat wave.
_____ sensitive to others' feelings; compassionate	E.) Playing ball in the hot summer sun really made him PARCHed.
_____ oppressively hot	F.) The lawyer's SPECIOUS argument had the jury fooled until all the evidence was revealed.
_____ softened, reduced in volume	G.) One year's hottest fashions are often PASSÉ by the next year.
_____ wealth and luxury	H.) *Saturday Night Live* regularly LAMPOONs political personalities.
_____ false, though appearing to be true	I.) Nurses are known for their TENDER treatment of hospital patients.
_____ no longer fashionable; out-of-date	J.) People with yachts and mansions live in great OPULENCE.

Step 3: Write Sentences

For each word write two sentences that indicate you know the meaning of the word. Then read aloud quickly three times each set of sentences that came to you. If you hesitated before coming up with the sentences or had to look up a word, say each of those sentences six times and write the vocabulary word you are studying at least three times. You can write them anywhere—on the lines after the sentences, in the margin, or on a piece of paper—as long as you write them.

Word: ABRIDGE

Sentence 1:

_____

_____

Sentence 2:

_____

_____

Word: BELLICOSE

Sentence 1:

_____

_____

Sentence 2:

_____

_____

Word: CHARLATAN

Sentence 1:

_____

_____

Sentence 2:

_____

_____

Word: DOMESTICATED

Sentence 1:

_____

_____

Sentence 2:

_____

_____

Word: DROLL

Sentence 1:

_____

_____

Sentence 2:

_____

_____

Word: EXACERBATE

Sentence 1:

_____

_____

Sentence 2:

_____

_____

Word: GENRE

Sentence 1:

_____

_____

Sentence 2:

_____

_____

Word: HYPERBOLE

Sentence 1:

_____

_____

Sentence 2:

_____

_____

Word: INCENSED

Sentence 1:

_____

_____

Sentence 2:

_____

_____

Word: INFAMOUS

Sentence 1:

_____

_____

Sentence 2:

_____

_____

Word: LAMPOON

Sentence 1:

_____

_____

Sentence 2:

_____

_____

Word: MUTED

Sentence 1:

_____

_____

Sentence 2:

_____

_____

Word: OPULENCE

Sentence 1:

_____

_____

Sentence 2:

_____

_____

Word: PARCH

Sentence 1:

_____

_____

Sentence 2:

_____

_____

Word: PASSÉ

Sentence 1:

_____

_____

Sentence 2:

_____

_____

Word: PIQUANT

Sentence 1:

_____

_____

Sentence 2:

_____

_____

Word: SPECIOUS

Sentence 1:

_____

_____

Sentence 2:

_____

_____

Word: SULTRY

Sentence 1:

_____

_____

Sentence 2:

_____

_____

Word: TENDER

Sentence 1:

_____

_____

Sentence 2:

_____

_____

Word: **TORPID**

Sentence 1:

_____

_____

Sentence 2:

_____

_____

If necessary, return and complete the crossword puzzle in Step I.

Puzzle 8

Step 1: Crossword Puzzle

Work on this crossword for no more than 15 minutes. If an answer does not occur to you after you've given it some thought, move on. It is possible that you will not complete the puzzle in the allotted time; it is not important that you do. What is important is that you work at it conscientiously for the full 15 minutes.

Across

1. NOT THINKING ABOUT THE FUTURE; SHORT-SIGHTED
6. Fourth scale note
7. OF POOR QUALITY OR WORKMANSHIP
9. HATE; DETEST
11. WORKABLE; DOABLE
14. Divulge*; reveal
16. Driver's lic. or Soc. Sec. card, for example: Abbr.
17. Gets ready to fire
19. LACKING FOOD, CLOTHING, AND SHELTER
20. Actress Sorvino
21. Twosome
24. State colonized by Oglethorpe: Abbr.
25. Celerity*; speed
26. STRONG, FIRM, UNCOMPROMISING
28. Judicious*; reasonable
29. Word of greeting
30. OVERBLOWN SPEECH; UNDUE USE OF EXAGGERATION

Down

2. Toy that has its ups and downs
3. PEACEFUL; CALM
4. Battle between nations
5. PUNISH WITH HARSH CRITICISM
6. Prevent the success of; impede*
8. MAKE A FORMAL SPEECH
10. SNEAKILY DANGEROUS OR HARMFUL
11. LONG, NARROW VIEW
12. POMPOUS IN SPEECH OR WRITING
13. HEAVENLY; OTHERWORLDLY
15. SUE IN COURT
18. Painting on a wall
21. Golfer's goal
22. "I can't believe ___!"
23. Computer operator
25. Tonsorial* concern
27. *Tommy* rock group, with "The"

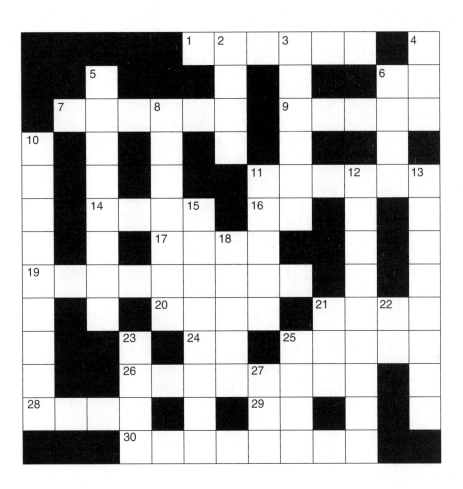

Step 2: Matching Columns

Work as long as necessary on these matching columns. Try to match every word with its definition. If you read carefully the sentences in which the words appear, you will in most cases be able to figure out the meaning of the words. Work diligently at figuring them out; it is a wonderful way to learn vocabulary. If there are words you cannot match, use the flashcards at the back of the book to complete this section. When you have finished, read through the matching columns four times. Each time you read the definition try to use the word in a new sentence. Slow down when you come to the word you're studying and write it. In this exercise, there's no need to write out the entire sentence or even the phrase in which it appears, unless you think that would help you remember the word.

DEFINITION	SAMPLE SENTENCE
_____ lacking food, clothing, and shelter	A.) His mother CHASTISEd him for skipping school to go swimming with his friends.
_____ punish with harsh criticism	B.) She got her homework done with CELERITY so she could go to the movies.
_____ prevent the success of; foil	C.) The preacher gave a BOMBASTIC sermon on the evils of graffiti.
_____ reveal, as a secret; tell	D.) She's so impatient that she ABHORs being behind slow drivers.
_____ pompous in speech or writing	E.) To avoid going to jail, he agreed to DIVULGE the gang's whereabouts.
_____ sneakily dangerous or harmful	F.) In olden days, politicians DECLAIMed on street corners.
_____ heavenly; otherworldly	G.) Nowadays, many a DESTITUTE person can be seen sleeping on city streets.
_____ hate; detest	H.) The mood music for the sci-fi film had an ETHEREAL quality about it.
_____ make a formal speech	I.) His quick action IMPEDEd the robbery long enough for the police to show up.
_____ speed; haste	J.) Terrorists are INSIDIOUS enemies; one never knows what they're up to until something happens.

DEFINITION	SAMPLE SENTENCE
_____ strong; firm; uncompromising	A.) Many feel that ignoring global warming is MYOPIC.
_____ not thinking about the future; short-sighted	B.) She has always been a STALWART supporter of equal rights.
_____ pertaining to barbers or barbering	C.) It took a while before the engineers could come up with a VIABLE solution to the problem.
_____ workable; doable	D.) The photographer captured perfectly the VISTA between the rows of trees.
_____ sue in court	E.) Because she was not emotionally involved in the dispute, she found it easy to make a JUDICIOUS decision.
_____ overblown speech; undue use of exaggeration	F.) When friendly conversations with his partner didn't lead to setting their financial disagreement, he had to LITIGATE.
_____ long, narrow view	G.) The remote lakeside was especially PLACID on that warm summer day.
_____ peaceful; calm	H.) In many small towns, the TONSORIAL shop is still a place where men socialize while waiting for their haircuts.
_____ reasonable; sane	I.) Because the carpenter was rushed, he did a SHODDY job on the bookcases he built.
_____ of poor quality or workmanship	J.) Politicians are known for their RHETORIC.

Step 3: Write Sentences

For each word write two sentences that indicate you know the meaning of the word. Then read aloud quickly three times each set of sentences that came to you. If you hesitated before coming up with the sentences or had to look up a word, say each of those sentences six times and write the vocabulary word you are studying at least three times. You can write them anywhere—on the lines after the sentences, in the margin, or on a piece of paper—as long as you write them.

Word: **ABHOR**

Sentence 1:

_____

_____

Sentence 2:

_____

_____

Word: **BOMBASTIC**

Sentence 1:

_____

_____

Sentence 2:

_____

_____

Word: CELERITY

Sentence 1:

_____

_____

Sentence 2:

_____

_____

Word: CHASTISE

Sentence 1:

_____

_____

Sentence 2:

_____

_____

Word: DECLAIM

Sentence 1:

_____

_____

Sentence 2:

_____

_____

Word: DESTITUTE

Sentence 1:

_____

_____

Sentence 2:

_____

_____

Word: DIVULGE

Sentence 1:

_____

_____

Sentence 2:

_____

_____

Word: ETHEREAL

Sentence 1:

_____

_____

Sentence 2:

_____

_____

Word: IMPEDE

Sentence 1:

_____

_____

Sentence 2:

_____

_____

Word: INSIDIOUS

Sentence 1:

_____

_____

Sentence 2:

_____

_____

Word: JUDICIOUS

Sentence 1:

_____

_____

Sentence 2:

_____

_____

Word: LITIGATE

Sentence 1:

_____

_____

Sentence 2:

_____

_____

Word: MYOPIC

Sentence 1:

_____

_____

Sentence 2:

_____

_____

Word: PLACID

Sentence 1:

_____

_____

Sentence 2:

_____

_____

Word: RHETORIC

Sentence 1:

_____

_____

Sentence 2:

_____

_____

Word: SHODDY

Sentence 1:

_____

_____

Sentence 2:

_____

_____

Word: STALWART

Sentence 1:

_____

_____

Sentence 2:

_____

_____

Word: TONSORIAL

Sentence 1:

_____

_____

Sentence 2:

_____

_____

Word: VIABLE

Sentence 1:

_____

_____

Sentence 2:

_____

_____

Word: VISTA

Sentence 1:

_____

_____

Sentence 2:

_____

_____

If necessary, return and complete the crossword puzzle in Step I.

Puzzle 9

Step 1: Crossword Puzzle

Work on this crossword for no more than 15 minutes. If an answer does not occur to you after you've given it some thought, move on. It is possible that you will not complete the puzzle in the allotted time; it is not important that you do. What is important is that you work at it conscientiously for the full 15 minutes.

Across

1. Cry very hard
4. Mischievous kid
7. TRUTHFULNESS
10. DISCOURAGE FROM ACTING
13. WEIRD AND MYSTERIOUS
15. Modern alternative to a VCR
16. RING LOUDLY
17. "This ___ not a test!"
18. SPECIFY FORMALLY, ESPECIALLY IN A CONTRACT
19. STOCKPILE OR HIDING PLACE
23. HINTED AT, BUT NOT DIRECTLY EXPRESSED
24. Facetious* or clever person
25. INSULTING
27. Happy ___ a lark
28. PLACE SIDE BY SIDE

Down

1. River of Paris
2. Place for surgery: Abbr.
3. DULL, ESPECIALLY DUE TO OVERFAMILIARITY
4. "Take ___ or leave ___!"
5. ___ *Big Fat Greek Wedding*
6. QUALITY OF BEING BRIEF AND TO THE POINT
8. INBORN; NATURAL
9. MOODY AND IRRITABLE
11. Note after la
12. Flower with thorns
13. At bat
14. INDIFFERENT, UNCARING, THOUGHTLESS
18. Frequent* the mall
20. CHEAP, GAUDY AND SHOWY
21. APPROACH OR GREET AGGRESSIVELY
22. USELESS; PRODUCING NO RESULT
26. MAKE SERIOUS DEMANDS ON; PUT A BURDEN ON

Step 2: Matching Columns

Work as long as necessary on these matching columns. Try to match every word with its definition. If you read carefully the sentences in which the words appear, you will in most cases be able to figure out the meaning of the words. Work diligently at figuring them out; it is a wonderful way to learn vocabulary. If there are words you cannot match, use the flashcards at the back of the book to complete this section. When you have finished, read through the matching columns four times. Each time you read the definition try to use the word in a new sentence. Slow down when you come to the word you're studying and write it. In this exercise, there's no need to write out the entire sentence or even the phrase in which it appears, unless you think that would help you remember the word.

DEFINITION	SAMPLE SENTENCE
_____ quality of being brief and to the point	A.) Even without radar, a police car parked at the side of the road can DETER speeders.
_____ discourage from acting	B.) When you have only a few minutes to tell a story, BREVITY is necessary.
_____ indifferent; uncaring; thoughtless	C.) She FREQUENTs antique shops in order to add to her collection.
_____ tongue-in-cheek; joking	D.) Jokes tend to become BANAL once you've heard them a few times.
_____ approach or greet aggressively	E.) The thief finally revealed where he had hidden his CACHE of stolen goods.
_____ visit often	F.) The player's CAVALIER attitude about missing practice got him kicked off the team.
_____ dull, especially due to over-familiarity	G.) He was always being FACETIOUS, so when he was finally serious no one believed him.
_____ insulting	H.) Since he knew nothing about carpentry, his attempts to fix the deck were FUTILE.
_____ useless; producing no result	I.) When he began making DEROGATORY remarks about how she hung the curtains, she finally told him to hang them himself.
_____ stockpile or hiding place	J.) The instant I walked into the store I was ACCOSTed by a salesman.

DEFINITION	SAMPLE SENTENCE
_____ make serious demands on; put a burden on	A.) It is necessary to STIPULATE the interest rate in a loan contract.
_____ specify formally, especially in a contract	B.) Her dad didn't have to say anything; it was IMPLICIT in his expression that he was angry with her for coming home too late.
_____ weird and mysterious	C.) The chapel bells PEALed to mark the start of the service.
_____ ring loudly	D.) Musical talent was clearly INNATE in the Bach family; every one of them was a first-class musician.
_____ cheap, gaudy, and showy	E.) The psychic's ability to make accurate predictions was UNCANNY.
_____ hinted at, but not directly expressed	F.) Since the witness was a friend of the accused, the lawyer doubted the VERACITY of his testimony.
_____ place side by side	G.) She had terrible taste in furniture; she always chose such TAWDRY patterns.
_____ truthfulness	H.) When she corrected the exams, the teacher JUXTAPOSEd each student's paper with the answer sheet.
_____ moody and irritable	I.) Her constant complaining began to TAX his patience.
_____ inborn; natural	J.) She was so spoiled that she became PETULANT over the most unimportant things.

Step 3: Write Sentences

For each word write two sentences that indicate you know the meaning of the word. Then read aloud quickly three times each set of sentences that came to you. If you hesitated before coming up with the sentences or had to look up a word, say each of those sentences six times and write the vocabulary word you are studying at least three times. You can write them anywhere—on the lines after the sentences, in the margin, or on a piece of paper—as long as you write them.

Word: ACCOST

Sentence 1:

_____

_____

Sentence 2:

_____

_____

Word: BANAL

Sentence 1:

_____

_____

Sentence 2:

_____

_____

Word: BREVITY

Sentence 1:

_____

_____

Sentence 2:

_____

_____

Word: CACHE

Sentence 1:

_____

_____

Sentence 2:

_____

_____

Word: CAVALIER

Sentence 1:

_____

_____

Sentence 2:

_____

_____

Word: DEROGATORY

Sentence 1:

_____

_____

Sentence 2:

_____

_____

Word: DETER

Sentence 1:

_____

_____

Sentence 2:

_____

_____

Word: FACETIOUS

Sentence 1:

_____

_____

Sentence 2:

_____

_____

Word: FREQUENT (v.)

Sentence 1:

_____

_____

Sentence 2:

_____

_____

Word: FUTILE

Sentence 1:

_____

_____

Sentence 2:

_____

_____

Word: IMPLICIT

Sentence 1:

_____

_____

Sentence 2:

_____

_____

Word: INNATE

Sentence 1:

_____

_____

Sentence 2:

_____

_____

Word: JUXTAPOSE

Sentence 1:

_____

_____

Sentence 2:

_____

_____

Word: PEAL

Sentence 1:

_____

_____

Sentence 2:

_____

_____

Word: PETULANT

Sentence 1:

_____

_____

Sentence 2:

_____

_____

Word: STIPULATE

Sentence 1:

_____

_____

Sentence 2:

_____

_____

Word: TAWDRY

Sentence 1:

_____

_____

Sentence 2:

_____

_____

Word: TAX (v.)

Sentence 1:

_____

_____

Sentence 2:

_____

_____

Word: UNCANNY

Sentence 1:

_____

_____

Sentence 2:

_____

_____

Word: VERACITY

Sentence 1:

_____

_____

Sentence 2:

_____

_____

If necessary, return and complete the crossword puzzle in Step I.

Puzzle 10

Step 1: Crossword Puzzle

Work on this crossword for no more than 15 minutes. If an answer does not occur to you after you've given it some thought, move on. It is possible that you will not complete the puzzle in the allotted time; it is not important that you do. What is important is that you work at it conscientiously for the full 15 minutes.

Across

1. ONE WHO HATES PEOPLE
10. "____ 'em, Rover!"
11. Profane* expression
13. BURDENSOME; LABORIOUS
15. Aunt in *The Wizard of Oz*
17. DECEIVE, TRICK OR MISLEAD
19. Speediness
21. Dry ____ a bone
22. DECEPTION; TRICKERY
25. Paternal* people
27. DEVELOP GRADUALLY
28. E pluribus ____
29. Append*
30. MINOR WEAKNESS OR FAULT
31. BLAND; DULL

Down

2. Prefix with metric
3. Transgression*
4. Adept* individual
5. Also
6. SNOBBISH; ARROGANT
7. Entitlements: Abbr.
8. Exclamation of surprise
9. POLITE WORD USED INSTEAD OF AN OFFENSIVE ONE
12. TERRIBLE FAILURE OR DISASTER
14. Express contrition* for
16. CAUSE TO COORDINATE OR INTERLOCK
18. Make a sudden thrust, as with a sword
20. WASTE
23. HARD AND UNFEELING
24. REPEAL OR ABOLISH
25. Composed of two parts
26. Fiasco*; failure; debacle

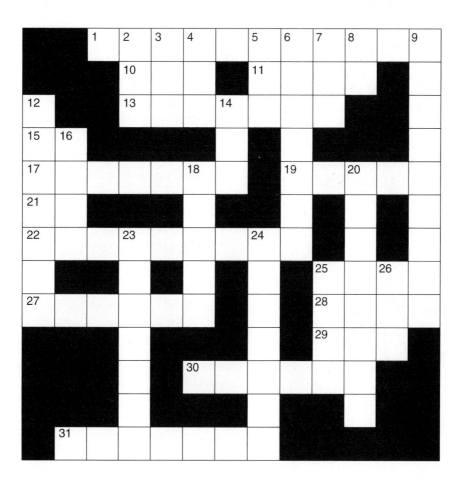

Step 2: Matching Columns

Work as long as necessary on these matching columns. Try to match every word with its definition. If you read carefully the sentences in which the words appear, you will in most cases be able to figure out the meaning of the words. Work diligently at figuring them out; it is a wonderful way to learn vocabulary. If there are words you cannot match, use the flashcards at the back of the book to complete this section. When you have finished, read through the matching columns four times. Each time you read the definition try to use the word in a new sentence. Slow down when you come to the word you're studying and write it. In this exercise, there's no need to write out the entire sentence or even the phrase in which it appears, unless you think that would help you remember the word.

DEFINITION	SAMPLE SENTENCE
_____ sincere remorse	A.) The clever thief BEGUILEd his victims with his smooth talking.
_____ failure; dud	B.) The teacher suspected CHICANERY when supplies continued to disappear from the classroom.
_____ develop gradually	C.) Because the lead singer was just getting over laryngitis, the concert was a FIASCO.
_____ skilled	D.) Rather than retype the whole contract, the lawyer APPENDed the new provisions on an extra page.
_____ add	E.) "Dang" and "crikey" are EUPHEMISMs for swear words that might offend some people.
_____ deception; trickery	F.) Our decision to go to the mountains last weekend EVOLVEd from dad's remark that we hadn't been skiing in a while.
_____ polite word used instead of an offensive one	G.) She felt CONTRITION over hurting her friend's feelings, and swore she'd never do it again.
_____ deceive, trick, or mislead	H.) The CALLOUS man showed no emotion when he broke up with his girlfriend.
_____ hard and unfeeling	I.) The stock market crash of 1987, when stocks lost almost 25 percent of their value in one day, was truly a DEBACLE for investors.
_____ terrible failure or disaster	J.) After assisting a carpenter all summer, Fred became quite ADEPT at woodwork.

DEFINITION	SAMPLE SENTENCE
_____ irreligious; vulgar	A.) Building a stone wall on our property proved to be an ONEROUS task.
_____ bland; dull	B.) They all thought he was perfect, but I knew he had FOIBLEs like all of us.
_____ sin	C.) She gave me a very HAUGHTY look when I said I didn't like the color of her Rolls Royce.
_____ minor weakness or fault	D.) Prohibition—the ban on alcoholic beverages—proved to be unworkable, and was RESCINDed in the 1930s.
_____ one who hates people	E.) She confessed her TRANSGRESSIONs every week at church.
_____ repeal or abolish	F.) When the reporter asked some tough questions, the politician's response included a few PROFANE words the newspaper couldn't print.
_____ snobbish; arrogant	G.) They tried to MESH their vacation plans so they could go away together.
_____ fatherlike	H.) They were so excited about being on vacation that they SQUANDERed all their money on the first day.
_____ cause to coordinate or interlock	I.) The network aired some new exciting shows to replace ones that viewers felt were INSIPID.
_____ burdensome; laborious	J.) After my father passed away, my uncle took a PATERNAL interest in me.
_____ waste	K.) The MISANTHROPE built himself a cabin deep in the woods, miles from the nearest person.

Step 3: Write Sentences

For each word write two sentences that indicate you know the meaning of the word. Then read aloud quickly three times each set of sentences that came to you. If you hesitated before coming up with the sentences or had to look up a word, say each of those sentences six times and write the vocabulary word you are studying at least three times. You can write them anywhere—on the lines after the sentences, in the margin, or on a piece of paper—as long as you write them.

Word: ADEPT

Sentence 1:

_____

_____

Sentence 2:

_____

_____

Word: APPEND

Sentence 1:

_____

_____

Sentence 2:

_____

_____

Word: BEGUILE

Sentence 1:

_____

_____

Sentence 2:

_____

_____

Word: CALLOUS

Sentence 1:

_____

_____

Sentence 2:

_____

_____

Word: CHICANERY

Sentence 1:

_____

_____

Sentence 2:

_____

_____

Word: CONTRITION

Sentence 1:

_____

_____

Sentence 2:

_____

_____

Word: DEBACLE

Sentence 1:

_____

_____

Sentence 2:

_____

_____

Word: EUPHEMISM

Sentence 1:

_____

_____

Sentence 2:

_____

_____

Word: EVOLVE

Sentence 1:

_____

_____

Sentence 2:

_____

_____

Word: FOIBLE

Sentence 1:

_____

_____

Sentence 2:

_____

_____

Word: HAUGHTY

Sentence 1:

_____

_____

Sentence 2:

_____

_____

Word: INSIPID

Sentence 1:

_____

_____

Sentence 2:

_____

_____

Word: MESH

Sentence 1:

_____

_____

Sentence 2:

_____

_____

Word: ONEROUS

Sentence 1:

_____

_____

Sentence 2:

_____

_____

Word: PATERNAL

Sentence 1:

_____

_____

Sentence 2:

_____

_____

Word: PROFANE

Sentence 1:

_____

_____

Sentence 2:

_____

_____

Word: RESCIND

Sentence 1:

_____

_____

Sentence 2:

_____

_____

Word: SQUANDER

Sentence 1:

_____

_____

Sentence 2:

_____

_____

Word: TRANSGRESSION

Sentence 1:

_____

_____

Sentence 2:

_____

_____

If necessary, return and complete the crossword puzzle in Step I.

Puzzle 11

Step 1: Crossword Puzzle

Work on this crossword for no more than 15 minutes. If an answer does not occur to you after you've given it some thought, move on. It is possible that you will not complete the puzzle in the allotted time; it is not important that you do. What is important is that you work at it conscientiously for the full 15 minutes.

Across

1. UNPREDICTABLE
5. The Beatles' "Let It ___"
6. SCOLD
8. Repeated practice to improve proficiency*
10. Gangster Capone
12. IMPENETRABLE BY LIGHT
14. Basketball official
15. LOWLY AND DEGRADING
16. Public relations: Abbr.
17. Symbol for copper
18. HARDSHIP; SEVERITY OF LIVING CONDITIONS
20. Adorable
22. HONOR OR RECOGNITION FOR SOMETHING WELL DONE
24. EASILY ANGERED
25. The Colonel's company
26. GREAT HAPPINESS AND JOY

Down

2. Place to get an ale
3. BITTERLY MOCKING OR SARCASTIC
4. Vociferous* cry
5. OBVIOUS IN A DEFIANT WAY
7. Dr. Dre's music
9. SHY OR QUIET
11. THRIFTY; ECONOMICAL
12. "___ course" ("Sure!")
13. Month known for precipitation*
16. DULL; ORDINARY
17. Massachusetts Cape
19. SOCIALLY UNREFINED
21. MYSTERY OR RIDDLE
23. Valiant* soldier
24. Viscous* fluid used in writing

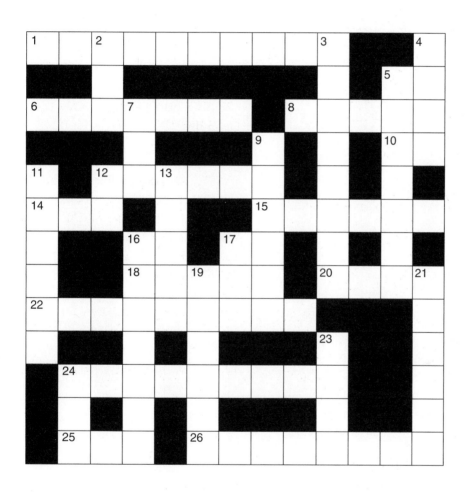

Step 2: Matching Columns

Work as long as necessary on these matching columns. Try to match every word with its definition. If you read carefully the sentences in which the words appear, you will in most cases be able to figure out the meaning of the words. Work diligently at figuring them out; it is a wonderful way to learn vocabulary. If there are words you cannot match, use the flashcards at the back of the book to complete this section. When you have finished, read through the matching columns four times. Each time you read the definition try to use the word in a new sentence. Slow down when you come to the word you're studying and write it. In this exercise, there's no need to write out the entire sentence or even the phrase in which it appears, unless you think that would help you remember the word.

DEFINITION	SAMPLE SENTENCE
_____ thrifty; economical	A.) It would be considered GAUCHE not to tip the host in a fine restaurant.
_____ lowly and degrading	B.) The Oscar-winning film won ACCOLADEs from all the critics.
_____ mystery or riddle	C.) Her behavior was so CAPRICIOUS that we never knew what to expect.
_____ obvious in a defiant way	D.) A feeling of EUPHORIA overcame her when she realized she'd won the lottery.
_____ honor or recognition for something well done	E.) His BLATANT lies didn't fool anyone.
_____ shy or quiet	F.) You probably wouldn't be so IRASCIBLE in traffic jams if you made sure to leave enough time to get to your destination.
_____ easily angered	G.) It's still an ENIGMA as to how ancient people built the giant statues on Easter Island.
_____ great happiness and joy	H.) Most would consider picking up garbage at the side of the road to be MENIAL work.
_____ unpredictable	I.) The DEMURE girl didn't say much when he tried to strike up a conversation.
_____ socially unrefined	J.) They lived such a FRUGAL life that despite their simple jobs they had managed to save over a million dollars by the time they retired.

DEFINITION	SAMPLE SENTENCE
_____ skill; expertness	A.) We are so used to modern comforts that it's hard to imagine what the RIGORs of pioneer life must have been like.
_____ dull; ordinary	B.) Motor oil is a VISCOUS fluid.
_____ brave; courageous	C.) A hush fell over the room when we heard this VOCIFEROUS cry.
_____ sticky; thick	D.) So many plots for movies nowadays are PROSAIC; can't they think of anything new?
_____ hardship; severity of living conditions	E.) Despite being vastly outnumbered, Davy Crockett and the other soldiers fought a VALIANT battle at the Alamo.
_____ wet weather; rain, snow, sleet, etc.	F.) The marchers' PROFICIENCY improved steadily due to their daily drills.
_____ loud; noisy	G.) Her parents severely UPBRAIDed her for coming home at 2 A.M.
_____ bitterly mocking or sarcastic	H.) We couldn't see through the window because it was made of OPAQUE glass.
_____ scold	I.) There was a great deal of flooding last spring due to unusual amounts of PRECIPITATION.
_____ impenetrable by light	J.) He couldn't keep friends for very long because he was so prone to making SARDONIC comments to them.

Step 3: Write Sentences

For each word write two sentences that indicate you know the meaning of the word. Then read aloud quickly three times each set of sentences that came to you. If you hesitated before coming up with the sentences or had to look up a word, say each of those sentences six times and write the vocabulary word you are studying at least three times. You can write them anywhere—on the lines after the sentences, in the margin, or on a piece of paper—as long as you write them.

Word: ACCOLADE

Sentence 1:

_____

_____

Sentence 2:

_____

_____

Word: BLATANT

Sentence 1:

_____

_____

Sentence 2:

_____

_____

Word: CAPRICIOUS

Sentence 1:

_____

_____

Sentence 2:

_____

_____

Word: DEMURE

Sentence 1:

_____

_____

Sentence 2:

_____

_____

Word: ENIGMA

Sentence 1:

_____

_____

Sentence 2:

_____

_____

Word: EUPHORIA

Sentence 1:

_____

_____

Sentence 2:

_____

_____

Word: FRUGAL

Sentence 1:

_____

_____

Sentence 2:

_____

_____

Word: GAUCHE

Sentence 1:

_____

_____

Sentence 2:

_____

_____

Word: IRASCIBLE

Sentence 1:

_____

_____

Sentence 2:

_____

_____

Word: MENIAL

Sentence 1:

_____

_____

Sentence 2:

_____

_____

Word: OPAQUE

Sentence 1:

_____

_____

Sentence 2:

_____

_____

Word: PRECIPITATION

Sentence 1:

_____

_____

Sentence 2:

_____

_____

Word: PROFICIENCY

Sentence 1:

_____

_____

Sentence 2:

_____

_____

Word: PROSAIC

Sentence 1:

_____

_____

Sentence 2:

_____

_____

Word: RIGOR

Sentence 1:

_____

_____

Sentence 2:

_____

_____

Word: SARDONIC

Sentence 1:

_____

_____

Sentence 2:

_____

_____

Word: UPBRAID

Sentence 1:

_____

_____

Sentence 2:

_____

_____

Word: VALIANT

Sentence 1:

_____

_____

Sentence 2:

_____

_____

Word: VISCOUS

Sentence 1:

_____

_____

Sentence 2:

_____

_____

Word: VOCIFEROUS

Sentence 1:

_____

_____

Sentence 2:

_____

_____

If necessary, return and complete the crossword puzzle in Step I.

Puzzle 12

Step 1: Crossword Puzzle

Work on this crossword for no more than 15 minutes. If an answer does not occur to you after you've given it some thought, move on. It is possible that you will not complete the puzzle in the allotted time; it is not important that you do. What is important is that you work at it conscientiously for the full 15 minutes.

Across

1. Solemn promise
4. DELICATE SKILL
7. OF RURAL LIFE OR SIMPLICITY
9. MISCHIEVOUS SPIRIT
10. Just in case
12. FINAL WARNING
13. SPREADING OUT OF CONTROL
16. "To ___, or not to...": Hamlet
17. DEDUCE FROM FACTS
20. 1982 Spielberg alien film
22. Smoke with a brown rapper
23. WANDERER
24. AUTHORITY GRANTED A RULER BY AN OVERWHELMING VOTE
26. EASE OF SPEAKING OR WRITING
27. Go in quest of*; search for

Down

1. WORD FOR WORD
2. FULL OF SAD LONGING
3. DRAW OUT
5. MAGNIFICENT; SUPERB
6. PRONOUNCE CLEARLY
8. DEPENDENT; SUBJECT TO
11. Resolute*; steadfast
14. HUMOROUS OR SATIRICAL IMITATION OF A SERIOUS WORK
15. Voluminous*
16. NONCHALANT; COOL
18. Handle, to a CBer
19. Actress Drescher of *The Nanny*, or the role she played
21. "Piggies," in a kids' rhyme
25. Raleigh is its capital: Abbr.

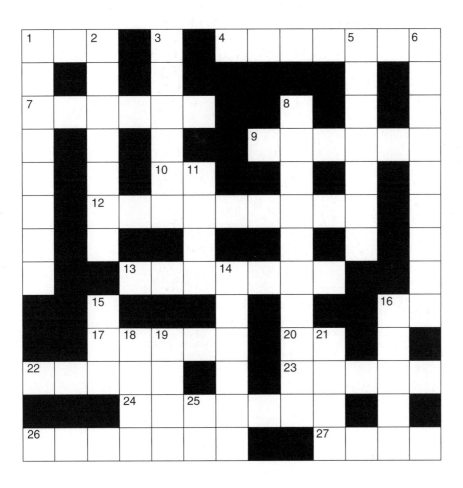

Step 2: Matching Columns

Work as long as necessary on these matching columns. Try to match every word with its definition. If you read carefully the sentences in which the words appear, you will in most cases be able to figure out the meaning of the words. Work diligently at figuring them out; it is a wonderful way to learn vocabulary. If there are words you cannot match, use the flashcards at the back of the book to complete this section. When you have finished, read through the matching columns four times. Each time you read the definition try to use the word in a new sentence. Slow down when you come to the word you're studying and write it. In this exercise, there's no need to write out the entire sentence or even the phrase in which it appears, unless you think that would help you remember the word.

DEFINITION	SAMPLE SENTENCE
_____ ease of speaking or writing	A.) The best teachers know how to ELICIT answers from students rather than just tell them.
_____ pronounce clearly	B.) The teacher became annoyed when the student acted BLASÉ about missing the test.
_____ dependent; subject to	C.) The negotiator used quite a bit of FINESSE to convince the two sides to compromise.
_____ wanderer	D.) His afternoon of golf was CONTINGENT on completing the company project by noon.
_____ authority granted a ruler by an overwhelming vote	E.) In ancient times, many NOMADs traveled from place to place in search of food.
_____ nonchalant; cool	F.) We had to ask her to repeat herself frequently because she didn't ENUNCIATE her words.
_____ deduce from facts	G.) Though he'd only been in the U.S. for two years, his FLUENCY in English was impressive.
_____ draw out	H.) It's fun to watch the little ones dress up as ghosts and GOBLINS on Halloween.
_____ delicate skill	I.) Many felt that the president's small margin of victory did not give him a MANDATE to raise taxes.
_____ mischievous spirit	J.) When the detective found that the car's engine was still warm, he INFERred that the suspect had gone out recently.

DEFINITION	SAMPLE SENTENCE
_____ final warning	A.) Many old New England towns have a RUSTIC look about them.
_____ full of sad longing	B.) Medieval knights often went on QUESTs to find the Holy Grail, a cup that supposedly had magical powers.
_____ humorous or satirical imitation of a serious work	C.) Even years later, she still became WISTFUL when she thought about her short-lived romance with Jim.
_____ word for word	D.) Because there are so many new players every year, *The Baseball Encyclopedia* has become quite a VOLUMINOUS book.
_____ of rural life or simplicity	E.) The mountain scenery in the Rockies is SUBLIME.
_____ very large, big	F.) The *Naked Gun* films are a PARODY of police movies.
_____ spreading out of control	G.) She was RESOLUTE in her decision to go to college, even if it meant borrowing money to pay tuition.
_____ steadfast in opinion; firm	H.) Mosquitoes tend to become RAMPANT in swampy areas.
_____ magnificent; superb	I.) He amazed the class by learning the Gettysburg Address VERBATIM in one night.
_____ search made in order to find something worthwhile	J.) The coach gave him an ULTIMATUM: if he missed any more practices, he'd be off the team.

Step 3: Write Sentences

For each word write two sentences that indicate you know the meaning of the word. Then read aloud quickly three times each set of sentences that came to you. If you hesitated before coming up with the sentences or had to look up a word, say each of those sentences six times and write the vocabulary word you are studying at least three times. You can write them anywhere—on the lines after the sentences, in the margin, or on a piece of paper—as long as you write them.

Word: BLASÉ

Sentence 1:

_____

_____

Sentence 2:

_____

_____

Word: CONTINGENT

Sentence 1:

_____

_____

Sentence 2:

_____

_____

Word: ELICIT

Sentence 1:

_____

_____

Sentence 2:

_____

_____

Word: ENUNCIATE

Sentence 1:

_____

_____

Sentence 2:

_____

_____

Word: FINESSE

Sentence 1:

_____

_____

Sentence 2:

_____

_____

Word: FLUENCY

Sentence 1:

_____

_____

Sentence 2:

_____

_____

Word: GOBLIN

Sentence 1:

_____

_____

Sentence 2:

_____

_____

Word: INFER

Sentence 1:

_____

_____

Sentence 2:

_____

_____

Word: MANDATE

Sentence 1:

_____

_____

Sentence 2:

_____

_____

Word: NOMAD

Sentence 1:

_____

_____

Sentence 2:

_____

_____

Word: PARODY

Sentence 1:

_____

_____

Sentence 2:

_____

_____

Word: QUEST

Sentence 1:

_____

_____

Sentence 2:

_____

_____

Word: RAMPANT

Sentence 1:

_____

_____

Sentence 2:

_____

_____

Word: RESOLUTE

Sentence 1:

_____

_____

Sentence 2:

_____

_____

Word: RUSTIC

Sentence 1:

_____

_____

Sentence 2:

_____

_____

Word: SUBLIME

Sentence 1:

_____

_____

Sentence 2:

_____

_____

Word: ULTIMATUM

Sentence 1:

_____

_____

Sentence 2:

_____

_____

Word: VERBATIM

Sentence 1:

_____

_____

Sentence 2:

_____

_____

Word: VOLUMINOUS

Sentence 1:

_____

_____

Sentence 2:

_____

_____

Word: WISTFUL

Sentence 1:

_____

_____

Sentence 2:

_____

_____

If necessary, return and complete the crossword puzzle in Step I.

Puzzle 13

Step 1: Crossword Puzzle

Work on this crossword for no more than 15 minutes. If an answer does not occur to you after you've given it some thought, move on. It is possible that you will not complete the puzzle in the allotted time; it is not important that you do. What is important is that you work at it conscientiously for the full 15 minutes.

Across

1. AMULET SUPPOSEDLY POSSESSING OCCULT POWERS
5. Pen filler
7. WORDY
9. TRACT OF LAND
10. HOLD BACK; HINDER
15. *Star Wars* princess
16. ABUNDANTLY PROVIDED (WITH)
17. *A ___ of Two Cities*
18. SEND AWAY TO ANOTHER COUNTRY
19. Hawaiian dance
22. Surgery reminder
23. LUCKY
24. Shakespeare's ___ *You Like It*
25. SPOTLESSLY CLEAN
27. Temporary craze; vogue*
28. Peruse*

Down

1. Golf gadget
2. INTRICATE MAZE
3. "Titanic" distress signal
4. ___ Dame University
6. START (A FIRE)
7. Vitality
8. "Phone home" alien
11. TEMPORARY INACTIVITY OR SUSPENSION
12. COPYING OR VIRTUALLY COPYING SOMEONE ELSE'S WORK
13. DESERVING ESTEEM; PRAISE-WORTHY
14. VAGUE, INDISTINCT
20. LEAVE SECRETLY, SO AS TO AVOID CAPTURE
21. INTOLERANT PERSON
23. QUICK, SUDDEN ATTACK
24. Help; succor*
26. TV hospital show

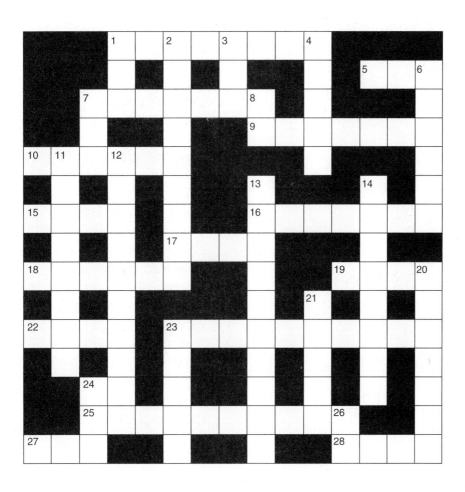

Step 2: Matching Columns

Work as long as necessary on these matching columns. Try to match every word with its definition. If you read carefully the sentences in which the words appear, you will in most cases be able to figure out the meaning of the words. Work diligently at figuring them out; it is a wonderful way to learn vocabulary. If there are words you cannot match, use the flashcards at the back of the book to complete this section. When you have finished, read through the matching columns four times. Each time you read the definition try to use the word in a new sentence. Slow down when you come to the word you're studying and write it. In this exercise, there's no need to write out the entire sentence or even the phrase in which it appears, unless you think that would help you remember the word.

DEFINITION	SAMPLE SENTENCE
_____ intolerant person	A.) She liked the hotel because the room was IMMACULATE when she arrived.
_____ vague, indistinct	B.) They held the decision in ABEYANCE until they had more information.
_____ lucky	C.) Her poetry was REPLETE with colorful images.
_____ wordy	D.) The wizard resorted to his TALISMAN when casting spells.
_____ spotlessly clean	E.) The city mayor asked the governor for SUCCOR after the hurricane hit.
_____ abundantly provided (with)	F.) The judge was a BIGOT who always ruled against minorities.
_____ help; aid	G.) Because his book report was twice as long as everyone else's, his teacher gave him a C for being VERBOSE.
_____ deserving esteem; praiseworthy	H.) It was FORTUITOUS that Jim's friend drove by just after Jim's car broke down; otherwise Jim would have had to walk home.
_____ temporary inactivity or suspension	I.) The rookie's CREDITABLE performance his first week won him a spot in the starting lineup.
_____ amulet supposedly possessing occult powers	J.) He had only a NEBULOUS memory of the events just before the accident.

DEFINITION	SAMPLE SENTENCE
_____ start (a fire); ignite; light up; arouse	A.) The bank teller ABSCONDed with the money.
_____ hold back; hinder	B.) The army unit's FORAY across enemy linescaught their opponents by surprise.
_____ exile; send away to another place or country	C.) The editor PERUSEd the article to check for errors.
_____ copying or virtually copying someone else's work	D.) It took a while to KINDLE the camp-fire because the wood was damp.
_____ temporary craze; fad	E.) The LABYRINTH of streets in the town made it hard to find one's way around.
_____ tract of land	F.) Fierce wind HAMPERed the fire-fighters' efforts to put out the blaze.
_____ quick, sudden attack; sudden excursion into enemy territory	G.) The writer of a book about a child wizard named Larry Trotter would almost certainly be guilty of PLAGIARISM.
_____ leave secretly so as to avoid capture	H.) The old leader was BANISHed when the new regime took over.
_____ read thoroughly	I.) The hilly TERRAIN made walking tiresome.
_____ intricate maze	J.) Miniskirts were the VOGUE in the sixties.

Step 3: Write Sentences

For each word write two sentences that indicate you know the meaning of the word. Then read aloud quickly three times each set of sentences that came to you. If you hesitated before coming up with the sentences or had to look up a word, say each of those sentences six times and write the vocabulary word you are studying at least three times. You can write them anywhere—on the lines after the sentences, in the margin, or on a piece of paper—as long as you write them.

Word: ABEYANCE

Sentence 1:

_____

_____

Sentence 2:

_____

_____

Word: ABSCOND

Sentence 1:

_____

_____

Sentence 2:

_____

_____

Word: BANISH

Sentence 1:

_____

_____

Sentence 2:

_____

_____

Word: BIGOT

Sentence 1:

_____

_____

Sentence 2:

_____

_____

Word: CREDITABLE

Sentence 1:

_____

_____

Sentence 2:

_____

_____

Word: FORAY

Sentence 1:

_____

_____

Sentence 2:

_____

_____

Word: FORTUITOUS

Sentence 1:

_____

_____

Sentence 2:

_____

_____

Word: HAMPER

Sentence 1:

_____

_____

Sentence 2:

_____

_____

Word: IMMACULATE

Sentence 1:

_____

_____

Sentence 2:

_____

_____

Word: KINDLE

Sentence 1:

_____

_____

Sentence 2:

_____

_____

Word: LABYRINTH

Sentence 1:

_____

_____

Sentence 2:

_____

_____

Word: NEBULOUS

Sentence 1:

_____

_____

Sentence 2:

_____

_____

Word: PERUSE

Sentence 1:

_____

_____

Sentence 2:

_____

_____

Word: PLAGIARISM

Sentence 1:

_____

_____

Sentence 2:

_____

_____

Word: REPLETE

Sentence 1:

_____

_____

Sentence 2:

_____

_____

Word: SUCCOR

Sentence 1:

_____

_____

Sentence 2:

_____

_____

Word: TALISMAN

Sentence 1:

_____

_____

Sentence 2:

_____

_____

Word: TERRAIN

Sentence 1:

_____

_____

Sentence 2:

_____

_____

Word: VERBOSE

Sentence 1:

_____

_____

Sentence 2:

_____

_____

Word: VOGUE

Sentence 1:

_____

_____

Sentence 2:

_____

_____

If necessary, return and complete the crossword puzzle in Step I.

Puzzle 14

Step 1: Crossword Puzzle

Work on this crossword for no more than 15 minutes. If an answer does not occur to you after you've given it some thought, move on. It is possible that you will not complete the puzzle in the allotted time; it is not important that you do. What is important is that you work at it conscientiously for the full 15 minutes.

Across

3. REVERED; ESTEEMED
6. FORMALLY ABOLISH; REPEAL
8. Author London
10. Pester; hector*
12. Not even
14. DIGRESSION; STRAYING FROM THE POINT
16. SPECTACULAR WINDFALL
18. BLAMEWORTHY
22. Actor/talk show host Danza
24. OMEN; SIGN
25. FRAGRANT

Down

1. DISPLAY BOLDLY OR DEFIANTLY
2. JOURNEY ON FOOT
3. Meat served parmigiana
4. Rhythmic musical genre*
5. INTENSIFY; MAGNIFY
7. THROW OVERBOARD TO IMPROVE STABILITY
9. DIFFICULT; INVOLVED
11. NOT GENUINE; FORGED
13. INADEQUATE SUPPLY; LACK
15. MAKE VOID; CANCEL
17. INDIRECT; NOT STRAIGHT
19. Computer key above "Shift"
20. Continuous pain; pang*
21. IRRITATE OR ANNOY
23. Miner's find

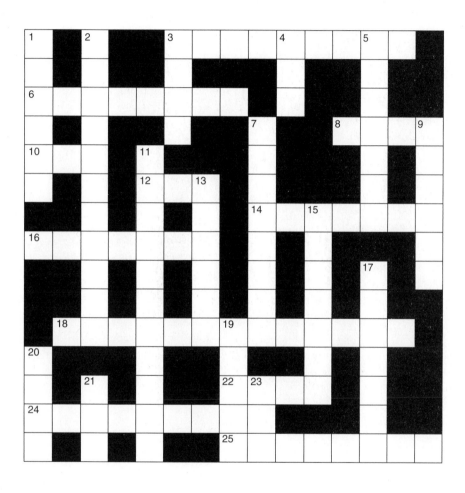

Step 2: Matching Columns

Work as long as necessary on these matching columns. Try to match every word with its definition. If you read carefully the sentences in which the words appear, you will in most cases be able to figure out the meaning of the words. Work diligently at figuring them out; it is a wonderful way to learn vocabulary. If there are words you cannot match, use the flashcards at the back of the book to complete this section. When you have finished, read through the matching columns four times. Each time you read the definition try to use the word in a new sentence. Slow down when you come to the word you're studying and write it. In this exercise, there's no need to write out the entire sentence or even the phrase in which it appears, unless you think that would help you remember the word.

DEFINITION	SAMPLE SENTENCE
_____ difficult; involved	A.) The DEARTH of natural resources in some countries severely slows industrial development.
_____ omen; sign	B.) Because he hadn't eaten since breakfast, he had hunger PANGs all afternoon.
_____ formally abolish; repeal	C.) Rap and jazz are two very different rhythmic musical GENREs.
_____ intensify; magnify	D.) It IRKed her to wait in line at the market.
_____ journey on foot	E.) How to master Rubik's Cube was a KNOTTY problem that none of us could solve.
_____ revered; esteemed	F.) Many old laws are ABROGATEd when they become outdated.
_____ continuous pain; ache	G.) Tomato and onions ENHANCE the flavor of a hamburger.
_____ irritate or annoy	H.) Melting snow and warming temperatures are HARBINGERs of spring.
_____ inadequate supply; lack	I.) The pope has always been a VENERATED religious leader.
_____ artistic or musical category	J.) Early settlers often had to PEREGRINATE for many miles to find food.

DEFINITION	SAMPLE SENTENCE
_____ display boldly or defiantly	A.) She FLAUNTed her wealth by wearing dazzling, expensive jewelry.
_____ not genuine; forged	B.) Their boat was in danger of sinking in the storm, so they had to JETTISON some supplies.
_____ indirect; not straight	C.) His home run was NULLIFied when they found out he used an illegal bat.
_____ nag; pester	D.) She was arrested for trying to use COUNTERFEIT bills at the supermarket.
_____ spectacular windfall	E.) Because some roads were closed by the storm, we had to take an OBLIQUE route to get to our destination.
_____ throw overboard to improve stability	F.) His unexpected inheritance was a BONANZA that enabled him to buy a mansion.
_____ fragrant	G.) It was hard to follow the lecture because the professor kept going off on a TANGENT.
_____ digression; straying from the point	H.) Her parents scolded her for her REPREHENSIBLE behavior.
_____ make void; cancel	I.) Her mom HECTORed her constantly about her messy room.
_____ blameworthy	J.) The bakery was REDOLENT with pleasant aromas.

Step 3: Write Sentences

For each word write two sentences that indicate you know the meaning of the word. Then read aloud quickly three times each set of sentences that came to you. If you hesitated before coming up with the sentences or had to look up a word, say each of those sentences six times and write the vocabulary word you are studying at least three times. You can write them anywhere—on the lines after the sentences, in the margin, or on a piece of paper—as long as you write them.

Word: ABROGATE

Sentence 1:

_____

_____

Sentence 2:

_____

_____

Word: BONANZA

Sentence 1:

_____

_____

Sentence 2:

_____

_____

Word: COUNTERFEIT

Sentence 1:

_____

_____

Sentence 2:

_____

_____

Word: DEARTH

Sentence 1:

_____

_____

Sentence 2:

_____

_____

Word: ENHANCE

Sentence 1:

_____

_____

Sentence 2:

_____

_____

Word: FLAUNT

Sentence 1:

_____

_____

Sentence 2:

_____

_____

Word: GENRE

Sentence 1:

_____

_____

Sentence 2:

_____

_____

Word: HARBINGER

Sentence 1:

_____

_____

Sentence 2:

_____

_____

Word: HECTOR

Sentence 1:

_____

_____

Sentence 2:

_____

_____

Word: IRK

Sentence 1:

_____

_____

Sentence 2:

_____

_____

Word: JETTISON

Sentence 1:

_____

_____

Sentence 2:

_____

_____

Word: KNOTTY

Sentence 1:

_____

_____

Sentence 2:

_____

_____

Word: NULLIFY

Sentence 1:

_____

_____

Sentence 2:

_____

_____

Word: OBLIQUE

Sentence 1:

_____

_____

Sentence 2:

_____

_____

Word: PANG

Sentence 1:

_____

_____

Sentence 2:

_____

_____

Word: PEREGRINATE

Sentence 1:

_____

_____

Sentence 2:

_____

_____

Word: REDOLENT

Sentence 1:

_____

_____

Sentence 2:

_____

_____

Word: REPREHENSIBLE

Sentence 1:

_____

_____

Sentence 2:

_____

_____

Word: TANGENT

Sentence 1:

_____

_____

Sentence 2:

_____

_____

Word: VENERATED

Sentence 1:

_____

_____

Sentence 2:

_____

_____

If necessary, return and complete the crossword puzzle in Step I.

Puzzle 15

Step 1: Crossword Puzzle

Work on this crossword for no more than 15 minutes. If an answer does not occur to you after you've given it some thought, move on. It is possible that you will not complete the puzzle in the allotted time; it is not important that you do. What is important is that you work at it conscientiously for the full 15 minutes.

Across

2. WITHDRAW INTO RETIREMENT; SECLUDE
6. MAJESTIC; HEROIC
9. STUBBORN; UNYIELDING
11. Scotsman's family
14. HURRY
16. Purple flower
17. CLOSING MUSICAL PASSAGE
18. CROUCH IN FEAR
19. ARTIFICIALLY GRAND OR IMPORTANT; POMPOUS
21. Beatles drummer
23. DELAY IN IMPENDING PUNISHMENT
24. Pealed*
25. BELIEVABLE; CREDIBLE
29. HAPPENING EVERY TWO YEARS
30. WITHERED; SHRIVELED

Down

1. INCISIVE; SHARP; BITING
3. Thigh muscle, for short
4. ADMIT TO CITIZENSHIP, ESPECIALLY WITH THE RIGHT TO VOTE
5. STALE; LACKING FRESHNESS OR ORIGINALITY
7. MOLD OR SHAPE TO FIT A SPECIFIC FORM
8. PUFFING UP, AS BY THE ACTION OF THE WIND
10. FELT THROUGH THE IMAGINED PARTICIPATION IN SOMEONE ELSE'S EXPERIENCE
12. Baton Rouge's state: Abbr.
13. Loose __ a goose
15. SUBTLE DIFFERENCE IN MEANING
16. ROUGH, JAGGED TEAR
20. RUINS; RUBBLE
22. "The doctor is __"
25. Geometry constant
26. Judge's field
27. Will Smith role
28. Took charge of

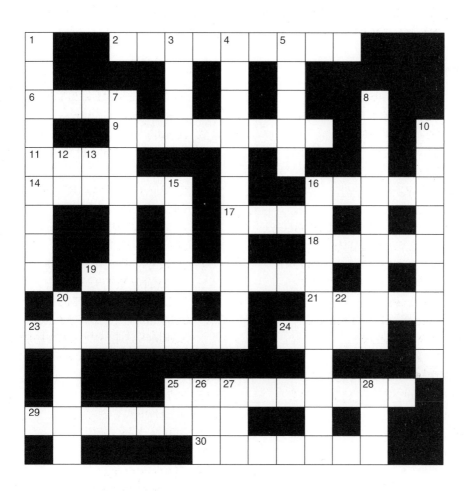

Step 2: Matching Columns

Work as long as necessary on these matching columns. Try to match every word with its definition. If you read carefully the sentences in which the words appear, you will in most cases be able to figure out the meaning of the words. Work diligently at figuring them out; it is a wonderful way to learn vocabulary. If there are words you cannot match, use the flashcards at the back of the book to complete this section. When you have finished, read through the matching columns four times. Each time you read the definition try to use the word in a new sentence. Slow down when you come to the word you're studying and write it. In this exercise, there's no need to write out the entire sentence or even the phrase in which it appears, unless you think that would help you remember the word.

DEFINITION	SAMPLE SENTENCE
_____ hurry	A.) Homer's *Iliad* is an example of an EPIC poem.
_____ ruins, rubble	B.) The dog would COWER in the corner whenever her owner scolded her.
_____ ring	C.) The jury convicted him because his attorney didn't present a PLAUSIBLE case for his innocence.
_____ puffing up; as by the action of the wind	D.) Sometimes juries are SEQUESTERed to keep them from having any contact with outsiders.
_____ subtle difference in meaning	E.) After the earthquake, they sifted through the DEBRIS looking for whatever belongings they could find.
_____ withered; shriveled	F.) We had to HASTEN to the theater to make the show on time.
_____ withdraw into retirement; seclude	G.) The church bells PEALed to announce the start of the service.
_____ majestic; heroic	H.) The flags were BILLOWING as the storm approached.
_____ crouch in fear	I.) Vocabulary words can be difficult to master when there are so many NUANCEs in meaning.
_____ believable; credible	J.) The Wicked Witch of the West was a WIZENED old woman.

DEFINITION	SAMPLE SENTENCE
_____ incisive; sharp; biting	A.) We tried to convince him not to buy the unreliable used car, but he was too OBDURATE to listen.
_____ delay in impending punishment	B.) The sharp edge of the paper caused a LACERATION to her finger.
_____ give the privileges of citizenship, particularly the right to vote	C.) The symphony ended with a dramatic CODA.
_____ mold or shape to fit a specific form	D.) He always started his speeches by telling TRITE old jokes.
_____ artificially showy or important; pompous	E.) Author Oscar Wilde was known for his TRENCHANT wit.
_____ happening every two years	F.) The suffrage movement in American resulted in women becoming ENFRANCHISEd.
_____ stubborn; unyielding	G.) Automobile seats are CONTOURed for passenger comfort.
_____ felt through the imagined participation in someone else's experience	H.) The candidate's GRANDIOSE speech offered empty solutions for the nation's problems.
_____ rough; jagged tear	I.) Many sports fans get VICARIOUS satisfaction from watching their heroes perform.
_____ closing musical passage	J.) The prisoner got a REPRIEVE when new evidence was presented in his case.
_____ stale; lacking freshness or originality	K.) The Olympic games are a BIENNIAL event.

Step 3: Write Sentences

For each word write two sentences that indicate you know the meaning of the word. Then read aloud quickly three times each set of sentences that came to you. If you hesitated before coming up with the sentences or had to look up a word, say each of those sentences six times and write the vocabulary word you are studying at least three times. You can write them anywhere—on the lines after the sentences, in the margin, or on a piece of paper—as long as you write them.

Word: BIENNIAL

Sentence 1:

_____

_____

Sentence 2:

_____

_____

Word: BILLOWING

Sentence 1:

_____

_____

Sentence 2:

_____

_____

Word: CODA

Sentence 1:

_____

_____

Sentence 2:

_____

_____

Word: CONTOUR

Sentence 1:

_____

_____

Sentence 2:

_____

_____

Word: COWER

Sentence 1:

_____

_____

Sentence 2:

_____

_____

Word: DEBRIS

Sentence 1:

_____

_____

Sentence 2:

_____

_____

Word: ENFRANCHISE

Sentence 1:

_____

_____

Sentence 2:

_____

_____

Word: EPIC

Sentence 1:

_____

_____

Sentence 2:

_____

_____

Word: GRANDIOSE

Sentence 1:

_____

_____

Sentence 2:

_____

_____

Word: HASTEN

Sentence 1:

_____

_____

Sentence 2:

_____

_____

Word: LACERATION

Sentence 1:

_____

_____

Sentence 2:

_____

_____

Word: NUANCE

Sentence 1:

_____

_____

Sentence 2:

_____

_____

Word: OBDURATE

Sentence 1:

_____

_____

Sentence 2:

_____

_____

Word: PEAL

Sentence 1:

_____

_____

Sentence 2:

_____

_____

Word: **PLAUSIBLE**

Sentence 1:

_____

_____

Sentence 2:

_____

_____

Word: **REPRIEVE**

Sentence 1:

_____

_____

Sentence 2:

_____

_____

Word: **SEQUESTER**

Sentence 1:

_____

_____

Sentence 2:

_____

_____

Word: TRENCHANT

Sentence 1:

_____

_____

Sentence 2:

_____

_____

Word: TRITE

Sentence 1:

_____

_____

Sentence 2:

_____

_____

Word: VICARIOUS

Sentence 1:

_____

_____

Sentence 2:

_____

_____

Word: WIZENED

Sentence 1:

_____

_____

Sentence 2:

_____

_____

If necessary, return and complete the crossword puzzle in Step I.

Crossword Puzzle Solutions

Puzzle 1

Puzzle 2

Puzzle 3

Puzzle 4

Puzzle 5

Puzzle 6

Puzzle 7

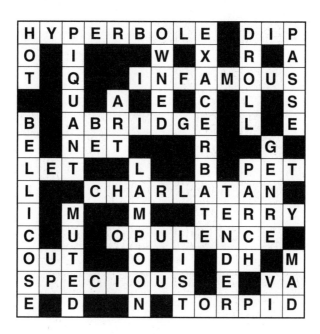

Puzzle 8

Puzzle 9

Puzzle 10

Puzzle 11

Puzzle 12

Puzzle 13

Puzzle 14

Puzzle 15

Overstudying

Matching Columns Set 2

As I mentioned earlier, it would be best if you could start on these thirty matching columns about two months before you take the SAT or other standardized test. You must try to complete four at each sitting. If you can, do them quickly; it will take seven days to finish the columns in this book. If you cannot complete four at a time, you should finish the remainder on the eighth or ninth day. The reason I'm setting a demanding schedule is because students who complete these matching columns two months before a test such as the SAT are more likely to use their newly acquired vocabulary when they write and as a result do better on the test.

While I recommend you complete Part 2 two months before taking the test, you may finish it any time you wish. A number of my students told me they moved on to Part 2 as soon as they finished Part 1. A majority of them told my people the reason they immediately went to work on Part 2 was because they didn't feel they had really mastered the vocabulary when they finished Part 1. I think, in some cases, they made the right decision. No matter when you completed Part 2, you should still read through these matching columns several times just before taking the test.

If the moment you read a definition the word pops into your mind and you can—without hesitation—use it in a sentence, you own that word. Nevertheless, you should repeat the word in context three times. Research shows that repeating it over and over, even when you know it cold, helps make it a permanent part of your vocabulary. If after reading the definition, you hesitate before coming up with the word or putting it in a sentence, look up the sentence we used. Read that sentence about a dozen times, each time slowing down and focusing on the word.

If you think you need to repeat this exercise before the SAT or other standardized test, do so. This time if the word occurs to you instantly, go to the next word. If you still have difficulty with a word, repeat it aloud in context a dozen times. If you continue to find it difficult to come up with many of the words, do not panic. All you have to do is repeat this exercise over and over until you are satisfied with your results. Sometimes spending more time overstudying has a built-in advantage. Often, those who have to spend more time learning words are far more likely to retain and use them than those who seem to learn new vocabulary words with little effort.

DEFINITION	SAMPLE SENTENCE
_____ weird and mysterious	A.) It is usually better to understand and forgive someone who hurts you than be VINDICTIVE.
_____ put oil on	B.) Because there are so many new players every year, *The Baseball Encyclopedia* has become quite a VOLUMINOUS book.
_____ give up one's position, office, or power	C.) He was brought to the emergency room suffering severe TRAUMA caused by the auto accident.
_____ truthfulness	D.) The psychic's ability to make accurate predictions was UNCANNY.
_____ lowly and degrading	E.) Heather LUBRICATEd the door to stop it from squeaking.
_____ too hard to cut, break or place	F.) Most would consider picking up garbage at the side of the road to be MENIAL work.
_____ inclined to seek revenge	G.) The MISANTHROPE built himself a cabin deep in the woods, miles from the nearest person.
_____ shock from a serious injury	H.) Without the right tools, he could not cut through the ADAMANTINE rock.
_____ one who hates people	I.) Since the witness was a friend of the accused, the lawyer doubted the VERACITY of his testimony.
_____ very large; big	J.) George was trying to lose weight, so he practiced ABSTINENCE when it came to eating fatty foods.
_____ the act of going without something	K.) The angry citizens forced the king to ABDICATE the throne.

DEFINITION	SAMPLE SENTENCE
_____ motivated purely by money	A.) He amazed the class by learning the Gettysburg Address VERBATIM in one night.
_____ understood by only a few	B.) Motor oil is a VISCOUS fluid.
_____ word for word	C.) Our dog has such a VORACIOUS appetite all the time that you'd think we never feed him.
_____ honor or recognition for something well done	D.) In many small towns, the TONSORIAL shop is still a place where men socialize while waiting for their haircuts.
_____ extremely hungry; almost impossible to satisfy	E.) In the '50s, the Rosenbergs were found guilty of TREASON for selling atom bomb secrets to the Russians.
_____ sticky; thick	F.) Her parents severely UPBRAIDed her for coming home at 2 A.M.
_____ hate; detest	G.) The _Scream_ film series contained many LURID scenes.
_____ pertaining to barbers or barbering	H.) She would not do anything for free; her motives were entirely MERCENARY.
_____ soothe or relieve	I.) When she suffered scrapes in a fall, her mom's tender loving care helped to MOLLIFY her discomfort.
_____ acting to overthrow one's government or ruler, or helping your country's enemy	J.) She's so impatient that she ABHORs being behind slow drivers.
_____ scold	K.) Advanced techniques of computer programming are quite ABSTRUSE.
_____ gruesome; horrible	L.) The Oscar-winning film won ACCOLADEs from all the critics.

DEFINITION	SAMPLE SENTENCE
_____ false, though appearing to be true	A.) The unhappy citizens wanted to DEPOSE the queen.
_____ develop gradually	B.) We endured a string of SULTRY days during the heat wave.
_____ to make worse; aggravate	C.) The old man's ECCENTRIC behavior made him an outcast in his town.
_____ remove from power	D.) The lawyer's SPECIOUS argument had the jury fooled until all the evidence was revealed.
_____ insulting	E.) Her CD collection was quite ECLECTIC, as it contained music from hip-hop to Celine Dion.
_____ make serious demands on; put a burden on	F.) Our decision to go to the mountains last weekend EVOLVEd from dad's remark that we hadn't been skiing in a while.
_____ oppressively hot	G.) When he kept making DEROGATORY remarks about how she hung the curtains, she finally told him to hang them himself.
_____ medical rehabilitation process	H.) Lying about why she missed the exam only EXACERBATEd the situation.
_____ person with a peculiar personality; screwball; nut	I.) To get rid of his student's lisp, the school counselor suggested speech THERAPY.
_____ made up of selections from various sources	J.) Her constant complaining began to TAX his patience.

DEFINITION	SAMPLE SENTENCE
_____ arrogant pride	A.) Surprisingly, Joanne seemed APATHETIC when told her mother was seriously ill.
_____ deception; trickery	B.) "We had to wait an eternity" is an example of HYPERBOLE.
_____ not thinking about the future; short-sighted	C.) The teacher suspected CHICANERY when supplies continued to disappear from the classroom.
_____ peaceful; charmingly simple	D.) Rather than retype the whole contract, the lawyer APPENDed the new provisions on an extra page.
_____ intentional exaggeration	E.) He enjoyed an IDYLLIC life on the small island.
_____ add	F.) Because of his HUBRIS, he truly expected to be voted the best-looking guy in the school.
_____ image, sometimes a sacred one	G.) She developed CHRONIC sneezing during allergy season.
_____ showing little or no emotion; cold	H.) When oil prices went up sharply due to a shortage, oil companies experienced a WINDFALL.
_____ unexpected gain or good fortune	I.) Many ICONs of saints and angels were on display in the church.
_____ occurring regularly over a long period	J.) Many feel that ignoring global warming is MYOPIC.

DEFINITION	SAMPLE SENTENCE
_____ softened; reduced in volume	A.) Night watchmen must learn to be VIGILANT no matter how tired they feel.
_____ brave; courageous	B.) A hush fell over the room when we heard his VOCIFEROUS cry.
_____ cheerful willingness; eagerness	C.) Though her political cartoons were focused on the issues, they were often WHIMSICAL as well.
_____ tiny	D.) Instead of discussing his own ideas, the politician launched into a TIRADE about his opponent's platform.
_____ ever awake and alert	E.) She confessed her TRANSGRESSIONs every week in church.
_____ approach or greet aggressively	F.) The coach gave him an ULTIMATUM; if he missed any more practices, he'd be off the team.
_____ loud, noisy	G.) Despite being vastly outnumbered, Davy Crockett and the other soldiers fought a VALIANT battle at the Alamo.
_____ authority granted a ruler by an overwhelming vote	H.) Many felt that the president's small margin of victory did not give him a MANDATE to raise taxes.
_____ free from blame	I.) Since it was cold out, he opened the window a MINUSCULE amount to let in some air.
_____ sin	J.) Even though their conversation was MUTED, the librarian asked them to stop talking.
_____ given to playful humor	K.) Peter was ABSOLVEd of guilt when John testified that the two of them were together on the night of the robbery.
_____ long, angry speech	L.) The instant I walked into the store I was ACCOSTed by a salesman.
_____ final warning	M.) She couldn't afford to buy a ticket, so she accepted the invitation to the concert with ALACRITY.

DEFINITION	SAMPLE SENTENCE
_____ dull; ordinary	A.) They DESECRATEd the church when they spray-painted graffiti on its wall.
_____ retreat to an earlier stage; progress backwards	B.) Because he was so DIFFIDENT, he couldn't bring himself to ask her to dance.
_____ stockpile or hiding place	C.) Rather than deal with the issues in the election, she made DISPARAGING remarks about her opponent.
_____ show disrespect for something holy or sacred	D.) It would be considered GAUCHE not to tip the host in a fine restaurant.
_____ shy; timid	E.) It's fun to watch the little ones dress up as ghosts and GOBLINS on Halloween.
_____ speed; haste	F.) In the duet, Sharon sang melody, while her partner Felicia sang HARMONY.
_____ sudden and significant	G.) So many plots for movies nowadays are PROSAIC; can't they think of anything new?
_____ quality of being brief and to the point	H.) When the company doubled the size of the factory, it achieved a QUANTUM increase in production.
_____ agreement; musical part that blends	I.) It's not healthy for an adult to REGRESS to childhood by crying and carrying on when he doesn't get what he wants.
_____ socially unrefined	J.) When you have only a few minutes to tell a story, BREVITY is necessary.
_____ mischievous spirit	K.) The thief finally revealed where he had hidden his CACHE of stolen goods.
_____ belittling or finding fault with	L.) She got her homework done with CELERITY so she could go to the movies.

DEFINITION		SAMPLE SENTENCE
_____ snobbish; arrogant	A.)	He felt DESPONDENT after losing the big game.
_____ clever verbal exchange; witty remarks	B.)	Her disappointing SAT scores DIMINISHed her chances of getting into the college of her choice.
_____ feeling of embarrassment or shame	C.)	To avoid going to jail, he agreed to DIVULGE the gang's whereabouts.
_____ feeling hopeless, dejected or very sad	D.)	Stephen King is a master of the horror GENRE.
_____ part that sticks out; bulge; bump	E.)	The candidates spoke GRANDILOQUENTLY in the debate.
_____ hard and unfeeling	F.)	She gave me a very HAUGHTY look when I said I didn't like the color of her Rolls Royce.
_____ speaking in a lofty style, as an orator	G.)	The tree trunk had a PROTUBERANCE where a branch had been mostly cut off.
_____ blunt or rough in manner	H.)	Medieval knights often went on QUESTs to find the Holy Grail, a cup that supposedly had magical powers.
_____ category or kind, as in an art form	I.)	The comedian came out on top in his REPARTEE with the heckler.
_____ search made in order to find something worthwhile	J.)	The clerk's replies became BRUSQUE when the customer kept asking the same questions.
_____ reveal; as a secret; tell	K.)	The CALLOUS man showed no emotion when he broke up with his girlfriend.
_____ lessen; reduce	L.)	He suffered CHAGRIN when he realized he'd forgotten his friend's birthday.

DEFINITION	SAMPLE SENTENCE
_____ tip to a waiter	A.) Nowadays, many a DESTITUTE person can be seen sleeping on city streets.
_____ repeal or abolish	B.) When the tornado destroyed their house they were truly in a DIRE situation.
_____ dreadful; terrible	C.) Tigers aren't DOMESTICATED, so they don't make good house pets.
_____ one pretending to have knowledge he really doesn't have; imposter	D.) In a debate, keep your answers GERMANE to the subject; don't bring up unrelated issues.
_____ unpredictable	E.) The recommended GRATUITY when dining out is 15 percent of the bill.
_____ tame	F.) The workers' strike at the factory led to a HIATUS in the work flow.
_____ sag or collapse under pressure	G.) It is PRUDENT not to walk in certain neighborhoods after dark.
_____ gap	H.) Mosquitoes tend to become RAMPANT in swampy areas.
_____ relevant; pertinent	I.) Prohibition—the ban on alcoholic beverages—proved to be unworkable, and was RESCINDED in the 1930s.
_____ wise in practical matters; sensible	J.) The bridge BUCKLEd because there were too many trucks on it.
_____ lacking food, clothing, and shelter	K.) Her behavior was so CAPRICIOUS that we never knew what to expect.
_____ spreading out of control	L.) When the new doctor continued to make incorrect diagnoses, we knew he was probably a CHARLATAN.

DEFINITION	SAMPLE SENTENCE
_____ sharply affecting one's sense of taste or smell; hot; peppery	A.) Even without radar, a police car parked at the side of the road can DETER speeders.
_____ indifferent; uncaring; thoughtless	B.) In the nasty political race, the two candidates made DISPARAGING remarks about each other's abilities.
_____ spoken with confidence, but not much thought	C.) The comedian delivered jokes in a DROLL monotone.
_____ reasonable; sensible	D.) The candidate's GLIB answers at the press conference cost him a lot of votes.
_____ punish with harsh criticism	E.) Young children are GULLIBLE and easy to fool.
_____ discourage from acting	F.) The city paid HOMAGE to the returning soldiers in the parade.
_____ oddly comical	G.) The PUNGENT onions made her cry when she was slicing them.
_____ respect or reverence given, as to a hero	H.) His patience and ability to consider all the angles helped him make RATIONAL decisions.
_____ inclined to believe anything; naïve	I.) John cleaned his shoes after the hike, but there was still a RESIDUE of mud on them.
_____ unfairly characterizing as unimportant	J.) We had to buy a new TV because ours was taken when the house was BURGLARIZEd.
_____ rob; steal from	K.) The player's CAVALIER attitude about missing practice got him kicked off the team.
_____ something that remains; remnant	L.) His mother CHASTISEd him for skipping school to go swimming with his friends.

DEFINITION	SAMPLE SENTENCE
_____ give implied approval to; overlook (something illegal)	A.) She was RESOLUTE in her decision to go to college, even if it meant borrowing money to pay tuition.
_____ not genuine or authentic; counterfeit	B.) To Muslims, Mecca is a SACRED place.
_____ make a formal speech	C.) A SCHISM has formed in some religious organizations over gay rights.
_____ steadfast in opinion; firm	D.) The best teachers know how to ELICIT answers from students rather than just tell them.
_____ specify formally, especially in contract	E.) We had to ask her to repeat herself frequently because she didn't ENUNCIATE her words.
_____ dedicated to some religious purpose; holy	F.) Barry Bonds has been an ESTIMABLE power hitter in the world of baseball.
_____ pronounce clearly	G.) We must never CONDONE the taking of hostages, no matter what the reason.
_____ separation in a group, especially due to a disagreement	H.) The spy was assigned to a COVERT operation.
_____ secret; undercover	I.) In olden days, politicians DECLAIMed on street corners.
_____ highest point	J.) Reports of UFOs over the town turned out to be SPURIOUS.
_____ worthy of esteem; excellent	K.) It is necessary to STIPULATE the interest rate in a loan contract.
_____ draw out	L.) At its ZENITH, the company made more computers than anyone else.

DEFINITION	SAMPLE SENTENCE
_____ unhappy; miserable	A.) Politicians are known for their RHETORIC.
_____ having a dreamlike quality	B.) Alone in the house, he felt TREPIDATION when the wind made the roof creak.
_____ heavenly; otherworldly	C.) If you SHIRK your homework, you won't get good grades.
_____ trembling fear	D.) Only found in Antarctica, the Adélie penguin is ENDEMIC to that region.
_____ occurring at regular intervals	E.) The outfielder's ERRANT throw went well over the catcher's head.
_____ magnificent; superb	F.) The mood music for the sci-fi film had an ETHEREAL quality about it.
_____ avoid a responsibility	G.) Wearing a Halloween costume on Valentine's Day would make you CONSPICUOUS.
_____ overblown speech; undue use of exaggeration	H.) The phases of the moon follow a CYCLICAL path.
_____ easily seen or noticed	I.) He never said he was DEJECTED, but we could tell from the way he moped all the time.
_____ restricted to a particular area	J.) They were so excited about being on vacation that they SQUANDERed all their money the first day.
_____ deviating from the proper course	K.) The mountain scenery in the Rockies is SUBLIME.
_____ waste	L.) Many horror movie scenes have an eerie, SURREAL quality about them.

DEFINITION	SAMPLE SENTENCE
_____ keep away from; shun	A.) When the lovers parted at the end of the film, it was a POIGNANT moment for the entire audience.
_____ deceive; trick	B.) We are so used to modern comforts that it's hard to imagine what the RIGORs of pioneer life must have been like.
_____ quiet; not inclined to talk	C.) He couldn't keep friends for very long because he was so prone to making SARDONIC comments to them.
_____ strongly affecting one's emotions	D.) Because the carpenter was rushed, he did a SHODDY job on the bookcase he built.
_____ hardship; severity of living conditions	E.) It's still an ENIGMA as to how ancient people built the giant statues on Easter Island.
_____ distrustful of the motives of others	F.) Her doctor told her to ESCHEW fatty foods.
_____ help; aid	G.) "Dang" and "crikey" are EUPHEMISMs for swear words that might offend some people.
_____ strong; firm; uncompromising	H.) His afternoon of golf was CONTINGENT on completing the company project by noon.
_____ mystery or riddle	I.) Some voters were CYNICAL of the shady politician's reasons for holding the fundraising dinner.
_____ dependent; subject to	J.) Shakespeare's villain Iago DELUDEd Othello into thinking he was his friend.
_____ bitterly mocking or sarcastic	K.) She has always been a STALWART supporter of equal rights.
_____ of poor quality or workmanship	L.) The community required SUCCOR from the government after the tornado hit.
_____ polite word used instead of an offensive one	M.) He was quite TACITURN at parties, making it difficult to have a conversation with him.

DEFINITION	SAMPLE SENTENCE
_____ terrible failure or disaster	A.) Many old New England towns have a RUSTIC look about them.
_____ adequate for the purpose; enough	B.) Only a SAVANT can truly understand the complexities of nuclear physics.
_____ person of profound learning; scholar	C.) The Easter service in honor of Christ was a SOLEMN event.
_____ great happiness and joy	D.) He ENTREATed the judge for mercy.
_____ cheap, gaudy, and showy	E.) A feeling of EUPHORIA overcame her when she realized she'd won the lottery.
_____ desolate; grim; harsh	F.) She felt CONTRITION over hurting her friend's feelings, and swore she'd never do it again.
_____ of rural life or simplicity	G.) The stock market crash of 1987, when stocks lost almost 25 percent of their value in one day, was truly a DEBACLE for investors.
_____ pray; beg	H.) The DEMURE girl didn't say much when he tried to strike up a conversation.
_____ sincere remorse	I.) The icy mountain was a STARK landscape for the climber.
_____ shy or quiet	J.) With only $5 in her pocket, she barely had a SUFFICIENT money to buy lunch.
_____ serious and dignified	K.) She had terrible taste in furniture; she always chose such TAWDRY patterns.

DEFINITION	SAMPLE SENTENCE
_____ place side by side	A.) She was so spoiled she became PETULANT over the most unimportant things.
_____ showing great intensity of spirit	B.) Modelers like to work with clay because it is a PLIANT material.
_____ stronghold; place of fortification	C.) The network put on some new exciting shows to replace ones that viewers felt were INSIPID.
_____ easy to bend; flexible	D.) When she corrected the exams, the teacher JUXTAPOSEd each student's paper with the answer sheet.
_____ ease of speaking or writing	E.) A gun is a LETHAL weapon.
_____ nonchalant; cool	F.) Good teamwork by the students EXPEDITEd the completion of their project.
_____ bland; dull	G.) The cheerleaders were FERVENT in their show of support for the team.
_____ person with power to decide; judge; referee	H.) Though he'd only been in the U.S. for two years, his FLUENCY in English was impressive.
_____ help speed things along	I.) The home plate umpire is the ARBITER of balls and strikes.
_____ fatal; deadly	J.) America is considered a great BASTION of freedom around the world.
_____ moody and irritable	K.) The teacher became annoyed when the student acted BLASÉ about missing the test.

DEFINITION	SAMPLE SENTENCE
_____ inappropriate light humor	A.) The chapel bells PEALed to mark the start of the service.
_____ obvious in a defiant way	B.) The salsa was so PIQUANT she thought her tongue would catch fire.
_____ failure; dud	C.) There was a great deal of flooding last spring due to unusual amounts of PRECIPITATION.
_____ destiny; fate	D.) The surprise party was such a well kept secret that she had no INTIMATION of what was about to happen.
_____ deceive, trick, or mislead	E.) My girl thinks we met because of KISMET; I think it was just coincidence.
_____ minor weakness or fault	F.) LEVITY at a funeral might not be appreciated by the deceased's family.
_____ old; from an earlier period	G.) The editor EXPUNGEd the unnecessary paragraph from the story.
_____ ring loudly	H.) Because the lead singer was just getting over laryngitis, the concert was a FIASCO.
_____ erase or strike out	I.) They all thought he was perfect, but I knew he had FOIBLES like all of us.
_____ wet weather; rain, snow, sleet, etc.	J.) Words like "thou" and "methinks" are considered ARCHAIC nowadays.
_____ hint; cue	K.) The clever thief BEGUILED his victims with his smooth talking.
_____ sharp to the taste	L.) His BLATANT lies didn't fool anyone.

DEFINITION	SAMPLE SENTENCE
_____ inclined to pick fights; quarrelsome	A.) They couldn't afford to take a trip this year because they were having PECUNIARY trouble.
_____ the quality of being genuine	B.) The remote lakeside was especially PLACID on that warm day.
_____ irreligious; vulgar	C.) You probably wouldn't be IRASCIBLE in traffic jams if you made sure to leave enough time to get to your destination.
_____ to make a mistake; err	D.) *Saturday Night Live* regularly LAMPOONs political personalities.
_____ delicate skill	E.) When the reporter asked some tough questions, the politician's response included a few PROFANE words the newspaper couldn't print.
_____ related to money	F.) The LIBERAL believed no one should be discriminated against because of race or sexual orientation.
_____ satirize; parody; poke fun at	G.) He was always being FACETIOUS, so when he finally got serious no one believed him.
_____ visit often	H.) The negotiator used quite a bit of FINESSE to convince the two sides to compromise.
_____ favoring political reform	I.) She FREQUENTs antique shops in order to add to her collection.
_____ peaceful; calm	J.) The Great Seal of the United States assures the AUTHENTICITY of paper money.
_____ easily angered	K.) The BELLICOSE leader constantly had his country on the brink of war.
_____ tongue-in-cheek; joking	L.) The planner BLUNDERed when he scheduled two games on the same field at the same time.

DEFINITION	SAMPLE SENTENCE
_____ make serious demands on; put a burden on	A.) Since he knew nothing about carpentry, his attempts to fix the deck were FUTILE.
_____ false, though appearing to be true	B.) He hurt her feelings by making BOORISH remarks about her painting.
_____ crude; insensitive	C.) He BRANDISHed the knife to frighten his attacker.
_____ medical rehabilitation process	D.) To get rid of his lisp, the school counselor suggested speech THERAPY.
_____ to make worse; aggravate	E.) The lawyer's SPECIOUS argument had the jury fooled until all the evidence was revealed.
_____ useless; producing no result	F.) Our decision to go to the mountains last weekend EVOLVEd from dad's remark that we hadn't been skiing in a while.
_____ sensitive to others' feelings; compassionate	G.) Lying about why she missed the exam only EXACERBATEd the situation.
_____ insulting	H.) The unhappy citizens wanted to DEPOSE the queen.
_____ shake or wave, as a weapon	I.) When he kept making DEROGATORY remarks about how she hung the curtains, she finally told him to hang them himself.
_____ remove from power	J.) Her constant complaining began to TAX his patience.
_____ bold in a rude way	K.) Nurses are known for their TENDER treatment of hospital patients.
_____ develop gradually	L.) The class was shocked at the BRAZEN remarks the student made to the teacher.

DEFINITION	SAMPLE SENTENCE
_____ burdensome; laborious	A.) Even years later, she still became WISTFUL when she thought about her short-lived romance with Jim.
_____ fatherlike	B.) When the rioters realized there was a shortage of police, they looted stores with IMPUNITY.
_____ sneakily dangerous or harmful	C.) Putting the rapper and the folk singer together in the same concert seemed INCONGRUOUS to us.
_____ exclude; banish	D.) Musical talent was clearly INNATE in the Bach family; every one of them was a first-class musician.
_____ wealth and luxury	E.) Terrorists are INSIDIOUS enemies; one never knows what they're up to until something happens.
_____ make extremely dry or thirsty	F.) The FBI tried to thwart his NEFARIOUS plan to blow up the building.
_____ inborn; natural	G.) Building a stone wall on our property proved to be an ONEROUS task.
_____ of unmatching parts; lacking harmony	H.) People with yachts and mansions live in great OPULENCE.
_____ full of sad longing	I.) When he continued to break the rules at the private club, he was finally OSTRACIZEd from it.
_____ extremely wicked or villainous	J.) Playing ball in the hot summer sun really made him PARCHed.
_____ complete freedom from punishment	K.) After my father passed away, my uncle took a PATERNAL interest in me.

DEFINITION	SAMPLE SENTENCE
_____ shorten or reduce	A.) The king was well-liked because of his BENIGN disposition.
_____ clever; skillful	B.) They lived such a FRUGAL life that despite their simple jobs they had managed to save over a million dollars.
_____ dull, especially due to overfamiliarity	C.) Because she was not emotionally involved in the dispute, she found it easy to make a JUDICIOUS decision.
_____ kind; good-natured disposition	D.) The disruptive student made FLIP-PANT remarks to the teacher.
_____ pompous in speech or writing	E.) Jokes tend to become BANAL once you've heard them a few times.
_____ distrustful of the motives of others	F.) The preacher gave a BOMBASTIC sermon on the evils of graffiti.
_____ forego; avoid	G.) Dictionaries are often ABRIDGEd to make them smaller and easier to use.
_____ very hungry	H.) Politicians not keeping their promises cause voters to be CYNICAL.
_____ disrespectful; irreverent	I.) If you're on a low-cholesterol diet, you should ESCHEW red meat.
_____ thrifty; economical	J.) After not eating all day, he was FAMISHED at dinner time.
_____ reasonable; sane	K.) After the heist the robber ADROITly eluded the police for weeks.

DEFINITION	SAMPLE SENTENCE
_____ feeling hopeless, dejected or very sad	A.) The New York Yankees' LEGACY of World Series victories may never be surpassed.
_____ impenetrable by light	B.) Her dad didn't have to say anything; it was IMPLICIT in his expression that he was angry with her for coming home too late.
_____ humorous or satirical imitation	C.) John's dad became INCENSED when he learned John had gotten a speeding ticket the first night he drove the family car.
_____ angry; mad	D.) Bonnie and Clyde were two of the most INFAMOUS criminals in modern history.
_____ snobbish; arrogant	E.) Unable to find any information that might damage his opponent, the politician resorted to insults and INNUENDOes.
_____ open to view; not secret	F.) In ancient times, many NOMADs traveled from place to place in search of food.
_____ reveal, as a secret; tell	G.) We couldn't see through the window because it was made of OPAQUE glass.
_____ something passed down to following generations	H.) Instead of holding it in, she showed OVERT anger by yelling and screaming.
_____ pleasant means of amusement or recreation	I.) The *Naked Gun* films are a PARODY of police movies.
_____ wanderer	J.) Baseball is our country's national PASTIME.
_____ having a negative reputation; famous for something bad	K.) He felt DESPONDENT after losing the big game.
_____ hinted at, but not directly expressed	L.) To avoid going to jail, he agreed to DIVULGE the gang's whereabouts.
_____ disparaging hint or implication	M.) She gave me a very HAUGHTY look when I said I didn't like the color of her Rolls Royce.

DEFINITION	SAMPLE SENTENCE
_____ central part around which other parts are gathered; core	A.) His quick action IMPEDEd the robbery long enough for the police to show up.
_____ lacking food, clothing, and shelter	B.) The IMPUDENT child publicly was rude to his father.
_____ cure-all	C.) When the detective found that the car's engine was still warm, he INFERred that the suspect had gone out recently.
_____ gap	D.) Listening to the old records evoked a feeling of NOSTALGIA in him.
_____ prevent the success of; foil	E.) A small group of friends formed the NUCLEUS of the club.
_____ relevant; pertinent	F.) We hang ORNAMENTAL lights on our Christmas tree each year.
_____ deduce from facts	G.) Scientists have yet to find a PANACEA for all ills.
_____ person with a peculiar personality; screwball; nut	H.) One year's hottest fashions are often PASSÉ by the next year.
_____ longing or sentimental feelings for the past	I.) Nowadays, many a DESTITUTE person can be seen sleeping on city streets.
_____ disrespectful in a bold way	J.) The old man's ECCENTRIC behavior made him an outcast in his town.
_____ decorative	K.) In a debate, keep your answers GERMANE to the subject; don't bring up unrelated issues.
_____ no longer fashionable; out-of-date	L.) The workers' strike at the factory led to a HIATUS in the work flow.

DEFINITION	SAMPLE SENTENCE
_____ made up of selections from various sources	A.) When friendly conversations with his partner did not settle their financial disagreement, he had to LITIGATE.
_____ of lofty dignity or imposing aspect	B.) It took a while before the engineers could come up with a VIABLE solution to the problem.
_____ sue in court	C.) Her CD collection was quite ECLECTIC, as it contained music from hip-hop to Celine Dion.
_____ workable; doable	D.) The mountains are a MAJESTIC sight.
_____ false, though appearing to be true	E.) The photographer captured perfectly the VISTA between the rows of trees.
_____ inclined to seek revenge	F.) The lawyer's SPECIOUS argument had the jury fooled until all the evidence was revealed.
_____ long, narrow view	G.) Motor oil is a VISCOUS fluid.
_____ wild and reckless	H.) After assisting a carpenter all summer, Fred became quite ADEPT at woodwork.
_____ sticky; thick	I.) The city tried to provide shelters for VAGRANTs so they wouldn't have to sleep on the streets.
_____ person who wanders with no employment or home; hobo	J.) He always felt TORPID during the hot summer months
_____ skilled	K.) It is usually better to understand and forgive someone who hurts you rather than be VINDICTIVE.
_____ inactive or sluggish	L.) The angry mob was responsible for WANTON destruction of store windows.

DEFINITION	SAMPLE SENTENCE
_____ ever awake and alert	A.) Nowadays, many a DESTITUTE person can be seen sleeping on city streets.
_____ show disrespect for something	B.) He felt DESPONDENT after losing the big game.
_____ discourage from acting	C.) Night watchmen must learn to be VIGILANT no matter how tired they feel.
_____ lacking food, clothing, and shelter	D.) They DESECRATEd the church when they spray-painted graffiti on its walls.
_____ feeling hopeless, dejected, or very sad	E.) Even without radar, a police car parked at the side of the road can DETER speeders.
_____ wild and reckless	F.) Her disappointing SAT scores DIMINISHed her chances of getting into a college of her choice.
_____ dreadful, terrible	G.) In the nasty political race, the two candidates made DISPARAGING remarks about each other's abilities.
_____ lessen; reduce	H.) Tigers aren't DOMESTICATED, so they don't make good house pets.
_____ shy; timid	I.) When the tornado destroyed their house, they were truly in a DIRE situation.
_____ unfairly characterizing as unimportant	J.) Because he was so DIFFIDENT, he couldn't bring himself to ask her to dance.
_____ tame	K.) The angry mob was responsible for WANTON destruction of store windows.

DEFINITION	SAMPLE SENTENCE
_____ steadfast in opinion; firm	A.) The marchers' PROFICIENCY improved steadily due to their daily drills.
_____ talk down to; treat as an inferior	B.) Politicians are known for their RHETORIC.
_____ of rural life or simplicity	C.) We are so used to modern comforts that it's hard to imagine what the RIGORs of pioneer life must have been like.
_____ skill; expertness	D.) My boss never treated the workers as equals; he seemed to enjoy PATRONIZing them instead.
_____ overblown speech; undue use of exaggeration	E.) Many old New England towns have a RUSTIC look about them.
_____ hardship; severity of living conditions	F.) She was RESOLUTE in her decision to go to college, even if it meant borrowing money to pay tuition.
_____ take more than your fair share	G.) Because she was a straight-A student, she had SANGUINE expectations about being accepted by a good college.
_____ serious and dignified	H.) Only a SAVANT can truly understand the complexities of nuclear physics.
_____ cheerfully optimistic	I.) To assure himself as much money as possible, the professional athlete planned to sign a long-term contract at the PINNACLE of his career.
_____ person of profound learning; scholar	J.) The Easter service in honor of Christ was a SOLEMN event.
_____ peak, top	K.) Whenever she was at a party with Jim, she MONOPOLIZED his attention.

DEFINITION	SAMPLE SENTENCE
_____ blameworthy	A.) Because some roads were closed by the storm, we had to take an OBLIQUE route to get to our destination.
_____ give the privileges of citizenship, particularly the right to vote	B.) Many sports fans get VICARIOUS satisfaction from watching their heroes perform.
_____ formally abolish; repeal	C.) The DEARTH of natural resources in some countries severely slows industrial development.
_____ start (a fire); ignite; light up; arouse	D.) The old leader was BANISHed when the new regime took over.
_____ happening every two years	E.) Her parents scolded her for her REPREHENSIBLE behavior.
_____ felt through the imagined participation in someone else's experience	F.) The suffrage movement in America resulted in women becoming ENFRANCHISEd.
_____ exile; send away to another place or country	G.) Many old laws were ABROGATEd when they became outdated.
_____ wordy	H.) It took a while to KINDLE the camp-fire because the wood was damp.
_____ indirect; not straight	I.) The Olympic games are a BIENNIAL event.
_____ inadequate supply; lack	J.) Because his book report was twice as long as everyone else's his teacher gave him a C for being VERBOSE.

DEFINITION	SAMPLE SENTENCE
_____ nag, pester	A.) The candidate's GRANDIOSE speech offered empty solutions for the nation's problems.
_____ copying or virtually copying someone else's work	B.) The rookie's CREDITABLE performance his first week won him a spot in the starting lineup.
_____ believable; credible	C.) The wizard resorted to his TALISMAN when casting spells.
_____ incisive; sharp; biting	D.) Early settlers often had to PEREGRINATE for many miles to find food.
_____ mold or shape to fit a specific form	E.) Her mom HECTORed her constantly about her messy room.
_____ make void; cancel	F.) The writer of a book about a child wizard named Larry Trotter would almost certainly be guilty of PLAGIARISM.
_____ artificially showy or important pompous	G.) The jury convicted him because his attorney didn't present a PLAUSIBLE case for his innocence.
_____ deserving esteem; praiseworthy	H.) Author Oscar Wilde was known for his TRENCHANT wit.
_____ journey on foot	I.) Automobile seats are CONTOURed for passenger comfort.
_____ amulet supposedly possessing occult powers	J.) Baseball authorities decided to NULLIFY his home run when they discovered he had used an illegal bat.

DEFINITION	SAMPLE SENTENCE
_____ throw overboard to improve stability	A.) After the earthquake, they sifted through the DEBRIS looking for whatever belongings they could find.
_____ ring	B.) The flags were BILLOWING as the storm approached.
_____ spotlessly clean	C.) The pope has always been a VENERATED religious leader.
_____ spectacular windfall	D.) The church bells PEALed to announce the start of the service.
_____ temporary inactivity or suspension	E.) He always started his speeches by telling TRITE old jokes.
_____ temporary craze; fad	F.) Their boat was in danger of sinking in the storm so they had to JETTISON some supplies.
_____ revered; esteemed	G.) She liked the hotel because the room was IMMACULATE when she arrived.
_____ ruins; rubble	H.) His unexpected inheritance was a BONANZA that enabled him to buy a mansion.
_____ stale; lacking freshness or originality	I.) They held the decision in ABEYANCE until they had more information.
_____ puffing up, as by the action of the wind	J.) Miniskirts were the VOGUE in the sixties.

DEFINITION	SAMPLE SENTENCE
_____ stubborn; unyielding	A.) She was arrested for trying to use COUNTERFEIT bills at the supermarket.
_____ withered; shriveled	B.) How to master Rubik's Cube was a KNOTTY problem that none of us could solve.
_____ display boldly or defiantly	C.) The bank teller ABSCONDed with the money.
_____ fragrant	D.) The dog would COWER in the corner whenever her owner scolded her.
_____ intricate maze	E.) The bakery was REDOLENT with pleasant aromas.
_____ help; aid	F.) We tried to convince him not to buy the unreliable used car, but he was too OBDURATE to listen.
_____ leave secretly; so as to avoid capture	G.) The Wicked Witch of the West was a WIZENED old woman.
_____ not genuine; forged	H.) The LABYRINTH of streets in the town made it hard to find one's way around.
_____ crouch in fear	I.) The city mayor asked the governor for SUCCOR after the hurricane hit.
_____ difficult; involved	J.) She FLAUNTed her wealth by wearing dazzling, expensive jewelry.

DEFINITION	SAMPLE SENTENCE
_____ omen; sign	A.) The editor PERUSEd the article to check for errors.
_____ lucky	B.) The judge was a BIGOT who always ruled against minorities.
_____ tract of land	C.) It was hard to follow the lecture because the professor kept going off on a TANGENT.
_____ hurry	D.) Vocabulary words can be difficult to master when there are so many NUANCEs in meaning.
_____ withdraw into retirement; seclude	E.) The symphony ended with a dramatic CODA.
_____ closing musical passage	F.) Melting snow and warming temperatures are HARBINGERs of spring.
_____ read thoroughly	G.) It was FORTUITOUS that Jim's friend drove by just after Jim's car broke down; otherwise Jim would have had to walk home.
_____ subtle difference in meaning	H.) The hilly TERRAIN made walking tiresome.
_____ digression; straying from the point	I.) We had to HASTEN to the theater to make the show on time.
_____ intolerant person	J.) Sometimes juries are SEQUESTERed to keep them from having any contact with outsiders.

DEFINITION	SAMPLE SENTENCE
_____ majestic; heroic	A.) Fierce wind HAMPERed the fire-fighters' efforts to put out the blaze.
_____ delay in impending punishment	B.) The army unit's FORAY across enemy lines caught their opponents by surprise.
_____ intensify; magnify	C.) Her poetry was REPLETE with colorful images.
_____ irritate or annoy	D.) Rap and jazz are two very different rhythmic musical GENREs.
_____ quick, sudden attack; sudden excursion into enemy territory	E.) Homer's *Iliad* is an example of an EPIC poem.
_____ vague, indistinct	F.) The sharp edge of the paper caused a LACERATION to her finger.
_____ continuous pain; ache	G.) The prisoner got a REPRIEVE when new evidence was presented in his case.
_____ hold back; hinder	H.) It IRKed her to wait in line at the market.
_____ abundantly provided (with)	I.) He had only a NEBULOUS memory of the events just before the accident.
_____ rough, jagged tear	J.) Tomato and onions ENHANCE the flavor of a hamburger.
_____ artistic or musical category	K.) Because he hadn't eaten since breakfast, he had hunger PANGs all afternoon.

Vocabulary Flashcards

How to Use the Flashcards

Step 1

Detach flashcards. After reading each definition, recall the word and put it in a sentence. If the word immediately pops into your head and you are able to use it in a sentence without hesitation, you own it.

Step 2

Divide the cards into two piles. In the first put the words you know instinctively; in the second, place the words you can define and put into sentences but only after working at it, along with the words you did not know.

Step 3

Go over those in the first pile three times, saying them aloud and putting them in sentences. Do the same for those in the second pile, only repeat the drill a dozen times, emphasizing and writing the word each time.

Step 4

After a short break go through all the cards very quickly. Any word you miss or have trouble putting in a sentence, place with the cards containing the words you missed.

Step 5

Go through all your cards three times two or three weeks before taking the SAT or other standardized test. Set aside the cards containing words you miss and look at them two or three days before the test. Do not study the night before; that's usually counterproductive. If you have worked at the exercises in this book, you have earned the right to feel that you have done all you can do and nobody can do more than that.

Good luck!

abdicate	abeyance
abhor	abridge
abrogate	abscond
absolve	abstinence

abeyance *(n.)* temporary inactivity or suspension

They held the decision in abeyance until they had more information.

abdicate *(v.)* give up one's position, office, or power

The angry citizens forced the king to abdicate the throne.

abridge *(v.)* shorten or reduce

Dictionaries are often abridged to make them smaller and easier to use.

abhor *(v.)* hate; detest

She's so impatient that she abhors being behind slow drivers.

abscond *(v.)* leave secretly so as to avoid capture

The bank teller absconded with the money.

abrogate *(v.)* formally abolish; repeal

Many old laws are abrogated when they become outdated.

abstinence *(n.)* the act of going without something

George was trying to lose weight, so he practiced abstinence when it came to eating fatty foods.

absolve *(v.)* free from blame

Peter was absolved of guilt when John testified that the two of them were together on the night of the robbery.

abstruse	**accolade**
accost	**adamantine**
adept	**adroit**
alacrity	**apathetic**

accolade *(n., usually plural)* honor or recognition for something well done

The Oscar-winning film won accolades from all the critics.

abstruse *(adj.)* understood by only a few

Advanced techniques of computer programming are quite abstruse.

adamantine *(adj.)* too hard to cut, break or pierce

Without the right tools, he could not cut through the adamantine rock.

accost *(v.)* approach or greet aggressively

The instant I walked into the store I was accosted by a salesman.

adroit *(adv./adj)* clever; skillful

After the heist, the robber adroitly eluded the police for weeks.

adept *(adj.)* skilled

After assisting a carpenter all summer, Fred became quite adept at woodwork.

apathetic *(adj.)* Showing little or no emotion; cold

Surprisingly, Joanne seemed apathetic when told her mother was seriously ill.

alacrity *(n.)* cheerful willingness; eagerness

She couldn't afford to buy a ticket, so she accepted the invitation to the concert with alacrity.

append	arbiter
archaic	authenticity
banal	banish
bastion	beguile

arbiter *(n.)* person with power to decide; judge; referee

The home plate umpire is the arbiter of balls and strikes.

append *(v.)* add

Rather than retype the whole contract, the lawyer appended the new provisions on an extra page.

authenticity *(n.)* the quality of being genuine

The Great Seal of the United States assures the authenticity of paper money.

archaic *(adj.)* old; from an earlier period

Words like "thou" and "methinks" are considered archaic nowadays.

banish *(v.)* exile; send away to another place or country

The old leader was banished when the new regime took over.

banal *(adj.)* dull, especially due to overfamiliarity

Jokes tend to become banal once you've heard them a few times.

beguile *(v.)* deceive, trick, or mislead

The clever thief beguiled his victims with his smooth talking.

bastion *(n.)* stronghold; place of great fortification

America is considered a great bastion of freedom around the world.

bellicose	benign
biennial	bigot
billowing	blasé
blatant	blunder

benign *(adj.)* kind; good-natured disposition

The king was well-liked because of his benign disposition.

bellicose *(adj.)* inclined to pick fights; quarrelsome

The bellicose leader constantly had his country on the brink of war.

bigot *(n.)* intolerant person

The judge was a bigot who always ruled against minorities.

biennial *(adj.)* happening every two years

The Olympic games are a biennial event.

blasé *(adj.)* nonchalant; cool

The teacher became annoyed when the student acted blasé about missing the test.

billowing *(v.)* puffing up, as by the action of the wind

The flags were billowing as the storm approached.

blunder *(v.)* to make a mistake; err

The planner blundered when he scheduled two games on the same field at the same time.

blatant *(adj.)* obvious in a defiant way

His blatant lies didn't fool anyone.

bombastic	bonanza
boorish	brandish
brazen	brevity
brusque	buckle

bonanza *(n.)* spectacular windfall

His unexpected inheritance was a bonanza that enabled him to buy a mansion.

bombastic *(adj.)* pompous in speech or writing

The preacher gave a bombastic sermon on the evils of graffiti.

brandish *(v.)* shake or wave, as a weapon

He brandished the knife to frighten his attacker.

boorish *(adj.)* crude; insensitive

He hurt her feelings by making boorish remarks about her painting.

brevity *(n.)* quality of being brief and to the point

When you have only a few minutes to tell a story, brevity is necessary.

brazen *(adj.)* bold in a rude way

The class was shocked at the brazen remarks the student made to the teacher.

buckle *(v.)* sag or collapse under pressure

The bridge buckled because there were too many trucks on it.

brusque *(adj.)* blunt or rough in manner

The clerk's replies became brusque when the customer kept asking the same questions.

burglarize	cache
callous	capricious
cavalier	celerity
chagrin	charlatan

cache *(n.)* stockpile or hiding place

The thief finally revealed where he had hidden his cache of stolen goods.

burglarize *(v.)* rob; steal from

We had to buy a new TV because ours was taken when the house was burglarized.

capricious *(adj.)* unpredictable

Her behavior was so capricious that we never knew what to expect.

callous *(adj.)* hard and unfeeling

The callous man showed no emotion when he broke up with his girlfriend.

celerity *(n.)* speed; haste

She got her homework done with celerity so she could go to the movies.

cavalier *(adj.)* indifferent; uncaring; thoughtless

The player's cavalier attitude about missing practice got him kicked off the team.

charlatan *(n.)* one pretending to have knowledge he doesn't really have; imposter

When the new doctor continued to make incorrect diagnoses, we knew he was probably a charlatan.

chagrin *(n.)* feeling of embarrassment or shame

He suffered chagrin when he realized he'd forgotten his friend's birthday.

chastise	chicanery
chronic	coda
condone	conspicuous
contingent	contour

chicanery *(n.)* deception; trickery

The teacher suspected chicanery when supplies continued to disappear from the classroom.

chastise *(v.)* punish with harsh criticism

His mother chastised him for skipping school to go swimming with his friends.

coda *(n.)* closing musical passage

The symphony ended with a dramatic coda.

chronic *(adj.)* occurring regularly over a long period

She developed chronic sneezing during the allergy season.

conspicuous *(adj.)* easily seen or noticed

Wearing a Halloween costume on Valentine's Day would make you conspicuous.

condone *(v.)* give implied approval to; overlook (something illegal)

We must never condone the taking of hostages, no matter what the reason.

contour *(v.)* mold or shape to fit a specific form

Automobile seats are contoured for passenger comfort.

contingent *(adj.)* dependent; subject to

His afternoon of golf was contingent on completing the company project by noon.

contrition	counterfeit
covert	cower
creditable	cyclical
cynical	dearth

counterfeit *(adj.)* not genuine; forged

She was arrested for trying to use counterfeit bills at the supermarket.

contrition *(n.)* sincere remorse

She felt contrition over hurting her friend's feelings, and swore she'd never do it again.

cower *(v.)* crouch in fear

The dog would cower in the corner whenever her owner scolded her.

covert *(adj.)* secret; undercover

The spy was assigned to a covert operation.

cyclical *(adj.)* occurring at regular intervals

The phases of the moon follow a cyclical pattern.

creditable *(adj.)* deserving esteem; praiseworthy

The rookie's creditable performance his first week won him a spot in the starting lineup.

dearth *(n.)* inadequate supply; lack

The dearth of natural resources in some countries severely slows industrial development.

cynical *(adj.)* distrustful of the motives of others

Some voters were cynical of the shady politician's reasons for holding the fundraising dinner.

debacle	debris
declaim	dejected
delude	demure
depose	derogatory

debris *(n.)* ruins; rubble

After the earthquake, they sifted through the debris looking for whatever belongings they could find.

debacle *(n.)* terrible failure or disaster

The stock market crash of 1987, when stocks lost almost 25 percent of their value in one day, was truly a debacle for investors.

dejected *(adj.)* unhappy; miserable

He never said he was dejected, but we could tell from the way he moped all the time.

declaim *(v.)* make a formal speech

In olden days, politicians declaimed on street corners.

demure *(adj.)* shy or quiet

The demure girl didn't say much when he tried to strike up a conversation.

delude *(v.)* deceive; trick

Shakespeare's villain Iago deluded Othello into thinking he was his friend.

derogatory *(adj.)* insulting

When he kept making derogatory remarks about how she hung the curtains, she finally told him to hang them himself.

depose *(v.)* remove from power

The unhappy citizens wanted to depose the queen.

desecrate	despondent
destitute	deter
diffident	diminish
dire	disparaging

despondent *(adj.)* feeling hopeless, dejected, or very sad

He felt despondent after losing the big game.

desecrate *(v.)* show disrespect for something holy or sacred

They desecrated the church when they spray-painted graffiti on its walls.

deter *(v.)* discourage from acting

Even without radar, a police car parked at the side of the road can deter speeders.

destitute *(adj.)* lacking food, clothing and shelter

Nowadays, many a destitute person can be seen sleeping on city streets.

diminish *(v.)* lessen; reduce

Her disappointing SAT scores diminished her chances of getting into the college of her choice.

diffident *(adj.)* shy; timid

Because he was so diffident, he couldn't bring himself to ask her to dance.

disparaging *(adj.)* belittling or finding fault with

Rather than deal with the issues in the election, she made disparaging remarks about her opponent.

dire *(adj.)* dreadful; terrible

When the tornado destroyed their house they were truly in a dire situation.

divulge	domesticated
droll	eccentric
eclectic	elicit
endemic	enfranchise

domesticated *(adj.)* tame

Tigers aren't domesticated, so they don't make good house pets.

divulge *(v.)* reveal, as a secret; tell

To avoid going to jail, he agreed to divulge the gang's whereabouts.

eccentric *(adj.)* person with a peculiar personality; screwball; nut

The old man's eccentric behavior made him an outcast in his town.

droll *(adj.)* oddly comical

The comedian delivered jokes in a droll monotone.

elicit *(v.)* draw out

The best teachers know how to elicit answers from students rather than just tell them.

eclectic *(adj.)* made up of selections from various sources

Her CD collection was quite eclectic, as it contained music from hip-hop to Celine Dion.

enfranchise *(v.)* give the privileges of citizenship, particularly the right to vote

The suffrage movement in America resulted in women becoming enfranchised.

endemic *(adj.)* restricted to a particular area

Only found in Antarctica, the Adélie penguin is endemic to that region.

enhance	enigma
entreat	enunciate
epic	errant
eschew	estimable

enigma *(n.)* mystery or riddle

It's still an enigma as to how ancient people built the giant statues on Easter Island.

enhance *(v.)* intensify; magnify

Tomato and onions enhance the flavor of a hamburger.

enunciate *(v.)* pronounce clearly

We had to ask her to repeat herself frequently because she didn't enunciate her words.

entreat *(v.)* pray; beg

He entreated the judge for mercy.

errant *(adj.)* deviating from the proper course

The outfielder's errant throw went well over the catcher's head.

epic *(adj.)* majestic; heroic

Homer's *Iliad* is an example of an epic poem.

estimable *(adj.)* worthy of esteem; excellent

Barry Bonds has been an estimable power hitter in the world of baseball.

eschew *(v.)* keep away from; shun

Her doctor told her to eschew fatty foods.

ethereal	euphemism
euphoria	evolve
exacerbate	expedite
expunge	facetious

euphemism *(n.)* polite word used instead of an offensive one

"Dang" and "crikey" are euphemisms for swear words that might offend some people.

---

ethereal *(adj.)* heavenly; otherwordly

The mood music for the sci-fi film had an ethereal quality about it.

---

evolve *(v.)* develop gradually

Our decision to go to the mountains last weekend evolved from dad's remark that we hadn't been skiing in a while.

---

euphoria *(n.)* great happiness and joy

A feeling of euphoria overcame her when she realized she'd won the lottery.

---

expedite *(v.)* help speed things along

Good teamwork by the students expedited the completion of their project.

---

exacerbate *(v.)* to make worse; aggravate

Lying about why she missed the exam only exacerbated the situation.

---

facetious *(adj.)* tongue-in-cheek; joking

He was always being facetious, so when he finally was serious no one believed him.

---

expunge *(v.)* erase or strike out

The editor expunged the unnecessary paragraph from the story.

famished	fervent
fiasco	finesse
flaunt	flippant
fluency	foible

fervent *(adj.)* showing great intensity of spirit; passionate; heated

The cheerleaders were fervent in their show of support for the team.

famished *(v.)* very hungry

After not eating all day, he was famished at dinnertime.

finesse *(n.)* delicate skill

The negotiator used quite a bit of finesse to convince the two sides to compromise.

fiasco *(n.)* failure; dud

Because the lead singer was just getting over laryngitis, the concert was a fiasco.

flippant *(adj.)* disrespectful; irreverent

The disruptive student made flip-pant remarks to the teacher.

flaunt *(v.)* display boldly or defiantly

She flaunted her wealth by wearing dazzling, expensive jewelry.

foible *(n.)* minor weakness or fault

They all thought he was perfect, but I knew he had foibles like all of us.

fluency *(n.)* ease of speaking or writing

Though he'd only been in the U.S. for two years, his fluency in English was impressive.

foray	fortuitous
frequent	frugal
futile	gauche
genre	germane

fortuitous *(adj.)* lucky

It was fortuitous that Jim's friend drove by just after Jim's car broke down; otherwise Jim would have had to walk home.

foray *(v.)* quick, sudden attack; sudden excursion into enemy territory

The army unit's foray across enemy lines caught their opponents by surprise.

frugal *(adj.)* thrifty; economical

They lived such a frugal life that despite their simple jobs they had managed to save over a million dollars by the time they retired.

frequent *(v.)* visit often

She frequents antique shops in order to add to her collection.

gauche *(adj.)* socially unrefined

It would be considered gauche not to tip the host in a fine restaurant.

futile *(adj.)* useless; producing no result

Since he knew nothing about carpentry, his attempts to fix the deck were futile.

germane *(adj.)* relevant; pertinent

In a debate, keep your answers germane to the subject; don't bring up unrelated issues.

genre *(n.)* category or kind, as in an art form

Rap and jazz are two very different rhythmic musical genres.

glib	goblin
grandiloquent	grandiose
gratuity	gullible
hamper	harbinger

goblin *(n.)* mischievous spirit

It's fun to watch the little ones dress up as ghosts and goblins on Halloween.

glib *(adj.)* spoken with confidence, but not much thought

The candidate's glib answers at the press conference cost him a lot of votes.

grandiose *(adj.)* artificially showy or important; pompous

The candidate's grandiose speech offered empty solutions for the nation's problems.

grandiloquent *(adj.; -ly adv.)* speaking in a lofty style, as an orator

The candidates spoke grandiloquently in the debate.

gullible *(adj.)* inclined to believe anything; naïve

Young children are gullible and easy to fool.

gratuity *(n.)* tip to a waiter

The recommended gratuity when dining out is 15 percent of the bill.

harbinger *(n.)* omen; sign

Melting snow and warming temperatures are harbingers of spring.

hamper *(v.)* hold back; hinder

Fierce wind hampered the firefighters' efforts to put out the blaze.

harmony	hasten
haughty	hector
hiatus	homage
hubris	hyperbole

hasten *(v.)* hurry

We had to hasten to the theater to make the show on time.

harmony *(n.)* agreement; musical part that blends with the melody

In the duet, Sharon sang melody, while her partner Felicia sang harmony.

hector *(v.)* nag; pester

Her mom hectored her constantly about her messy room.

haughty *(adj.)* snobbish; arrogant

She gave me a very haughty look when I said I didn't like the color of her Rolls Royce.

homage *(n.)* respect or reverence given, as to a hero

The city paid homage to the returning soldiers in the parade.

hiatus *(n.)* gap

The workers' strike at the factory led to a hiatus in the work flow.

hyperbole *(n.)* intentional exaggeration

"We had to wait an eternity" is an example of hyperbole.

hubris *(n.)* arrogant pride

Because of his hubris, he truly expected to be voted the best-looking guy in school.

icon	idyllic
immaculate	impede
implicit	impudent
impunity	incensed

idyllic *(adj.)* peaceful; charmingly simple

He enjoyed an idyllic life on the small island.

icon *(n.)* image, sometimes a sacred one

Many icons of saints and angels were on display in the church.

impede *(v.)* prevent the success of; foil

His quick action impeded the robbery long enough for the police to show up.

immaculate *(adj.)* spotlessly clean

She liked the hotel because the room was immaculate when she arrived.

impudent *(adj.)* disrespectful in a bold way

The impudent child publicly was rude to his father.

implicit *(adj.)* hinted at, but not directly expressed

Her dad didn't have to say anything; it was implicit in his expression that he was angry with her for coming home too late.

incensed *(vt.)* angry; mad

John's dad became incensed when he learned John had gotten a speeding ticket the first night he drove the family car.

impunity *(n.)* complete freedom from punishment

When the rioters realized there was a shortage of police, they looted stores with impunity.

incongruous	**infamous**
infer	**innate**
innuendo	**insidious**
insipid	**intimation**

infamous *(adj.)* having a negative reputation; famous for something bad

Bonnie and Clyde were two of the most infamous criminals in modern history.

incongruous *(adj.)* of unmatching parts; lacking harmony

Putting the rapper and the folk singer together in the same concert seemed incongruous to us.

innate *(adj.)* inborn; natural

Musical talent was clearly innate in the Bach family; every one of them was a first-class musician.

infer *(v.)* deduce from facts

When the detective found that the car's engine was still warm, he inferred that the suspect had gone out recently.

insidious *(adj.)* sneakily dangerous or harmful

Terrorists are insidious enemies; one never knows what they're up to until something happens.

innuendo *(n.)* disparaging implication about someone or something

Unable to find any information that might damage his opponent, the politician resorted to insults and innuendos.

intimation *(n.)* hint; cue

The surprise party was such a well kept secret that she had no intimation of what was about to happen.

insipid *(adj.)* bland; dull

The network aired some new exciting shows to replace ones that viewers felt were insipid.

irascible	irk
jettison	judicious
juxtapose	kindle
kismet	knotty

irk *(v.)* irritate or annoy

It irked her to wait in line at the market.

irascible *(adj.)* easily angered

You probably wouldn't be so irascible in traffic jams if you made sure to leave enough time to get to your destination.

judicious *(adj.)* reasonable; sane

Because she was not emotionally involved in the dispute, she found it easy to make a judicious decision.

jettison *(v.)* throw overboard to improve stability

Their boat was in danger of sinking in the storm, so they had to jettison some supplies.

kindle *(v.)* start (a fire); ignite; light up; arouse

It took a while to kindle the campfire because the wood was damp.

juxtapose *(v.)* place side by side

When she corrected the exams, the teacher juxtaposed each student's paper with the answer sheet.

knotty *(adj.)* difficult; involved

How to master Rubik's Cube was a knotty problem that none of us could solve.

kismet *(n.)* destiny; fate

My girlfriend thinks we met because of kismet; I think it was just coincidence.

labyrinth	laceration
lampoon	legacy
lethal	levity
liberal	litigate

laceration *(n.)* rough, jagged tear

The sharp edge of the paper caused a laceration to her finger.

labyrinth *(n.)* intricate maze

The labyrinth of streets in the town made it hard to find one's way around.

legacy *(n.)* something passed down to following generations

The New York Yankees' legacy of World Series victories may never be surpassed.

lampoon *(v.)* satirize; parody; poke fun at

Saturday Night Live regularly lampoons political personalities.

levity *(n.)* inappropriate light humor

Levity at a funeral might not be appreciated by the deceased's family.

lethal *(adj.)* fatal; deadly

A gun is a lethal weapon.

litigate *(v.)* sue in court

When friendly conversations with his partner didn't lead to settling their financial disagreement, he had to litigate.

liberal *(n.)* favoring political reform

The liberal believed no one should be discriminated against because of race or sexual orientation.

lubricate	lurid
majestic	mandate
menial	mercenary
mesh	minuscule

lurid *(adj.)* gruesome; horrible

The *Scream* film series contained many lurid scenes.

lubricate *(v.)* put oil on

Heather lubricated the door to stop it from squeaking.

mandate *(n.)* authority granted a leader by an overwhelming vote

Many felt that the president's small margin of victory did not give him a mandate to raise taxes.

majestic *(adj.)* of lofty dignity or imposing aspect

The mountains were a majestic sight when viewed from the nearby desert.

mercenary *(adj.)* motivated purely by money

She would not do anything for free; her motives were entirely mercenary.

menial *(adj.)* lowly and degrading

Most would consider picking up garbage at the side of the road to be menial work.

minuscule *(adj.)* tiny

Since it was cold out, he opened the window a minuscule amount to let in some air.

mesh *(v.)* cause to coordinate or interlock

They tried to mesh their vacation plans so they could go away together.

misanthrope	mollify
monopolize	muted
myopic	nebulous
nefarious	nomad

mollify *(v.)* sooth or relieve

When she suffered scrapes in a fall, her mom's tender loving care helped to mollify her discomfort.

misanthrope *(n.)* one who hates people

The misanthrope built himself a cabin deep in the woods, miles from the nearest person.

muted *(adj.)* softened; reduced in volume

Even though their conversation was muted, the librarian asked them to stop talking.

monopolize *(v.)* take more than your fair share; hog

Whenever she was at a party with Jim, she always monopolized his attention.

nebulous *(adj.)* vague, indistinct

He had only a nebulous memory of the events just before the accident.

myopic *(adj.)* not thinking about the future; short-sighted

Many feel that ignoring global warming is myopic.

nomad *(n.)* wanderer

In ancient times many nomads traveled from place to place in search of food.

nefarious *(adj.)* extremely wicked or villainous

The FBI tried to thwart his nefarious plan to blow up the building.

nostalgia	nuance
nucleus	nullify
obdurate	oblique
onerous	opaque

nuance *(n.)* subtle difference in meaning

Vocabulary words can be difficult to master when there are so many nuances in meaning.

nostalgia *(n.)* longing or sentimental feelings for the past

Listening to the old records evoked a feeling of nostalgia in him.

nullify *(v.)* make void; cancel

His home run was nullified when they found out he used an illegal bat.

nucleus *(n.)* central part around which other parts are gathered; core

A small group of friends formed the nucleus of the club.

oblique *(adj.)* indirect; not straight

Because some roads were closed by the storm, we had to take an oblique route to get to our destination.

obdurate *(adj.)* stubborn; unyielding

We tried to convince him not to buy the unreliable used car, but he was too obdurate to listen.

opaque *(adj.)* impenetrable by light

We couldn't see through the window because it was made of opaque glass.

onerous *(adj.)* burdensome; laborious

Building a stone wall on our property proved to be an onerous task.

opulence	ornamental
ostracize	overt
panacea	pang
parch	parody

ornamental *(adj.)* decorative

We hang ornamental lights on our Christmas tree each year.

opulence *(n.)* wealth and luxury

People with yachts and mansions live in great opulence.

overt *(adj.)* open to view; not secret

Instead of holding it in, she showed overt anger by yelling and screaming.

ostracize *(v.)* exclude; banish

When he continued to break the rules at the private club, he was finally ostracized from it.

pang *(n.)* continuous pain; ache

Because he hadn't eaten since breakfast, he had hunger pangs all afternoon.

panacea *(n.)* universal remedy

Scientists have yet to find a panacea for all ills.

parody *(n.)* humorous or satirical imitation of a serious work

The *Naked Gun* films are a parody of police movies.

parch *(vt.)* make extremely dry or thirsty

Playing ball in the hot summer sun really made him parched.

passé	pastime
paternal	patronize
peal	pecuniary
peregrinate	peruse

pastime *(n.)* pleasant means of amusement or recreation

Baseball is our country's national pastime.

passé *(adj.)* no longer fashionable; out-of-date

One year's hottest fashions are often passé by the next year.

patronize *(v.)* talk down to; treat as an inferior

My boss never treated the workers as equals; he seemed to enjoy patronizing them instead.

paternal *(adj.)* fatherlike

After my father passed away, my uncle took a paternal interest in me.

pecuniary *(adj.)* related to money

They couldn't afford to take a trip this year because they were having pecuniary trouble.

peal *(v.)* ring loudly

The chapel bells pealed to mark the start of the service.

peruse *(v.)* read thoroughly

The editor perused the article to check for errors.

peregrinate *(vt.)* journey on foot

Early settlers often had to peregrinate for many miles to find food.

petulant	pinnacle
piquant	placid
plagiarism	plausible
pliant	poignant

pinnacle *(n.)* peak; top

To assure himself as much money as possible, the professional athlete planned to sign a long-term contract at the pinnacle of his career.

petulant *(adj.)* moody and irritable

She was so spoiled that she became petulant over the most unimportant things.

placid *(adj.)* peaceful; calm

The remote lakeside was especially placid on that warm summer day.

piquant *(adj.)* sharp to the taste

The salsa was so piquant she thought her tongue would catch fire.

plausible *(adj.)* believable; credible

The jury convicted him because his attorney didn't present a plausible case for his innocence.

plagiarism *(n.)* copying or virtually copying someone else's work

The writer of a book about a child wizard named Larry Trotter would almost certainly be guilty of plagiarism.

poignant *(adj.)* strongly affecting one's emotions

When the lovers parted at the end of the film, it was a poignant moment for the entire audience.

pliant *(adj.)* easy to bed; flexible

Modelers like to work with clay because it's a pliant material.

precipitation	profane
proficiency	prosaic
protuberance	prudent
pungent	quantum

profane *(adj.)* irreligious; vulgar

When the reporter asked some tough questions, the politician's response included some profane words the newspaper couldn't print.

precipitation *(n.)* wet weather; rain, snow, sleet, etc.

There was a great deal of flooding last spring due to unusual amounts of precipitation.

prosaic *(adj.)* dull; ordinary

So many plots for movies nowadays are prosaic; can't they think of anything new?

proficiency *(n.)* skill; expertness

The marchers' proficiency improved steadily due to their daily drills.

prudent *(adj.)* wise in practical matters; sensible

It is prudent not to walk in certain neighborhoods after dark.

protuberance *(n.)* part that sticks out; bulge; bump

The tree trunk had a protuberance where a branch had been mostly cut off.

quantum *(adj.)* sudden and significant

When the company doubled the size of the factory, it achieved a quantum increase in production.

pungent *(adj.)* sharply affecting one's sense of taste or smell; hot; peppery

The pungent onions made her cry when she was slicing them.

quest	rampant
rational	redolent
regress	repartee
replete	reprehensible

rampant *(adj.)* spreading out of control

Mosquitoes tend to become rampant in swampy areas.

quest *(n.)* search made in order to find something worthwhile

Medieval knights often went on quests to find the Holy Grail, a cup that supposedly had magical powers.

redolent *(adj.)* fragrant

The bakery was redolent with pleasant aromas.

rational *(adj.)* reasonable; sensible

His patience and ability to consider all the angles helped him make rational decisions.

repartee *(n.)* clever verbal exchange; witty remarks

The comedian came out on top in his repartee with the heckler.

regress *(v.)* retreat to an earlier stage; progress backwards

It's not healthy for an adult to regress to childhood by crying and carrying on when he doesn't get what he wants.

reprehensible *(adj.)* blameworthy

Her parents scolded her for her reprehensible behavior.

replete *(adj.)* abundantly provided (with)

Her poetry was replete with colorful images.

reprieve	**rescind**
residue	**resolute**
rhetoric	**rigor**
rustic	**sacred**

rescind *(v.)* repeal or abolish

Prohibition—the ban on alcoholic beverages—proved to be unworkable, and was rescinded in the 1930s.

reprieve *(n.)* delay in impending punishment

The prisoner got a reprieve when new evidence was presented in his case.

resolute *(adj.)* steadfast in opinion; firm

She was resolute in her decision to go to college, even if it meant borrowing money to pay tuition.

residue *(n.)* something that remains; remnant

John cleaned his shoes after the hike, but there was still a residue of mud on them.

rigor *(n.)* hardship; severity of living conditions

We are so used to modern comforts that it's hard to imagine what the rigors of pioneer life must have been like.

rhetoric *(n.)* overblown speech; undue use of exaggeration

Politicians are known for their rhetoric.

sacred *(adj.)* dedicated to some religious purpose; holy

To Muslims, Mecca is a sacred place.

rustic *(adj.)* of rural life or simplicity

Many old New England towns have a rustic look about them.

sanguine	sardonic
savant	schism
sequester	shirk
shoddy	solemn

sardonic *(adj.)* bitterly mocking or sarcastic

He couldn't keep friends for very long because he was so prone to making sardonic comments to them.

sanguine *(adj.)* cheerfully optimistic

Because she was a straight-A student, she had sanguine expectations about being accepted by a good college.

schism *(n.)* separation in a group, especially due to a disagreement

A schism has formed in some religious organizations over gay rights.

savant *(n.)* person of profound learning; scholar

Only a savant can truly understand the complexities of nuclear physics.

shirk *(v.)* avoid a responsibility

If you shirk your homework, you won't get good grades.

sequester *(v.)* withdraw into retirement; seclude

Sometimes juries are sequestered to keep them from having any contact with outsiders.

solemn *(adj.)* serious and dignified

The Easter service in honor of Christ was a solemn event.

shoddy *(adj.)* of poor quality of workmanship

Because the carpenter was rushed, he did a shoddy job on the bookcases he built.

specious	spurious
squander	stalwart
stark	stipulate
sublime	succor

spurious *(adj.)* not genuine or authentic; counterfeit

Reports of UFOs over the town turned out to be spurious.

specious *(adj.)* false, though appearing to be true

The lawyer's specious argument had the jury fooled until all the evidence was revealed.

stalwart *(adj.)* strong, firm, uncompromising

She has always been a stalwart supporter of equal rights.

squander *(v.)* waste

They were so excited about being on vacation that they squandered all their money the first day.

stipulate *(v.)* specify formally, especially in a contract

It is necessary to stipulate the interest rate in a loan contract.

stark *(adj.)* desolate; grim; harsh

The icy mountain was a stark landscape for the climber.

succor *(n.)* help; aid

The community required succor from the government after the tornado hit.

sublime *(adj.)* magnificent; superb

The mountain scenery in the Rockies is sublime.

sufficient	sultry
surreal	taciturn
talisman	tangent
tawdry	tax

sultry *(adj.)* oppressively hot

We endured a string of sultry days during the heat wave.

---

sufficient *(adj.)* adequate for the

With only $5 in her pocket, she barely had sufficient money to buy lunch.

---

taciturn *(adj.)* quiet; not inclined to talk

He was quite taciturn at parties, making it difficult to have a conversation with him.

---

surreal *(adj.)* having a dreamlike quality

Many horror movie scenes have an eerie, surreal quality about them.

---

tangent *(n.)* digression; straying from the point

It was hard to follow the lecture because the professor kept going off on a tangent.

---

talisman *(n.)* amulet supposedly possessing occult powers

The wizard resorted to his talisman when casting spells.

---

tax *(v.)* make serious demands on; put a burden on

Her constant complaining began to tax his patience.

---

tawdry *(adj.)* cheap, gaudy, and showy

She had terrible taste in furniture; she always chose such tawdry patterns.

tender	terrain
therapy	tirade
tonsorial	torpid
transgression	trauma

terrain *(n.)* tract of land

The hilly terrain made walking tiresome.

tender *(adj.)* sensitive to others' feelings; compassionate

Nurses are known for their tender treatment of hospital patients.

tirade *(n.)* long, angry speech

Instead of discussing his own ideas, the politician launched into a tirade about his opponent's.

therapy *(n.)* medical rehabilitation process

To get rid of his lisp, the school counselor suggested speech therapy.

torpid *(adj.)* inactive or sluggish

He always felt torpid during the hot summer months.

tonsorial *(adj.)* pertaining to barbers or barbering

In many small towns, the tonsorial shop is still a place where men socialize while waiting for their haircuts.

trauma *(n.)* shock from a serious injury

He was brought to the emergency room suffering severe trauma from the auto accident.

transgression *(n.)* sin

She confessed her transgressions every week at church.

treason	trenchant
trepidation	trite
ultimatum	uncanny
upbraid	vagrant

trenchant *(adj.)* incisive; sharp; biting

Author Oscar Wilde was known for his trenchant wit.

treason *(n.)* acting to overthrow one's government or ruler, or helping your country's enemy

In the '50s, the Rosenbergs were found guilty of treason for selling atom bomb secrets to the Russians.

trite *(adj.)* stale; lacking freshness or originality

He always started his speeches by telling trite old jokes.

trepidation *(n.)* trembling fear

Alone in the house, he felt trepidation when the wind made the roof creak.

uncanny *(adj.)* weird and mysterious

The psychic's ability to make accurate predictions was uncanny.

ultimatum *(n.)* final warning

The coach gave him an ultimatum: if he missed any more practices, he'd be off the team.

vagrant *(n.)* person who wanders about with no employment or home; hobo

The city tried to provide shelters for vagrants so they wouldn't have to sleep on the streets.

upbraid *(v.)* scold

Her parents severely upbraided her for coming home at 2 A.M.

valiant	venerated
veracity	verbatim
verbose	viable
vicarious	vigilant

venerated *(adj.)* revered; esteemed

The pope has always been a venerated religious leader.

valiant *(adj.)* brave; courageous

Despite being vastly outnumbered, Davy Crockett and the other soldiers fought a valiant battle at the Alamo.

verbatim *(adv.)* word for word

He amazed the class by learning the Gettysburg Address verbatim in one night.

veracity *(n.)* truthfulness

Since the witness was a friend of the accused, the lawyer doubted the veracity of his testimony.

viable *(adj.)* workable; doable

It took a while before the engineers could come up with a viable solution to the problem.

verbose *(adj.)* wordy

Because his book report was twice as long as everyone else's, his teacher gave him a C for being verbose.

vigilant *(adj.)* ever awake and alert

Night watchmen must learn to be vigilant no matter how tired they feel.

vicarious *(adj.)* felt through the imagined participation in someone else's experience

Many sports fans get vicarious satisfaction from watching their heroes perform.

vindictive	viscous
vista	vociferous
vogue	voluminous
voracious	wanton

viscous *(adj.)* sticky; thick

Motor oil is a viscous fluid.

vindictive *(adj.)* inclined to seek revenge

It is usually better to understand and forgive someone who hurts you rather than be vindictive.

vociferous *(adj.)* loud; noisy

A hush fell over the room when we heard his vociferous cry.

vista *(n.)* long, narrow view

The photographer captured perfectly the vista between the rows of trees.

voluminous *(adj.)* very large; big

Because there are so many new players every year, *The Baseball Encyclopedia* has become quite a voluminous book.

vogue *(n.)* temporary craze; fad

Miniskirts were the vogue in the sixties.

wanton *(adj.)* wild and reckless

The angry mob was responsible for wanton destruction of store windows.

voracious *(adj.)* extremely hungry; almost impossible to satisfy

Our dog has such a voracious appetite all the time that you'd think we never feed him.

whimsical	windfall
wistful	wizened
zenith	

windfall *(n.)* unexpected gain or good fortune

When oil prices went up sharply due to a shortage, oil companies experienced a windfall.

whimsical *(adj.)* given to playful humor

Though her political cartoons were focused on the issues, they were often whimsical as well.

wizened *(adj.)* withered; shriveled

The Wicked Witch of the West was a wizened old woman.

wistful *(adj.)* full of sad longing

Even years later, she still became wistful when she thought about her short-lived romance with Jim.

zenith *(n.)* highest point

At its zenith, the company made more computers than anyone else.

AFTER THE TEST

Preparing for College was my first title for this section, but I changed it when I discovered that many of my students didn't read it. They thought since they had already taken the SAT and, in some cases, had been accepted into the college of their choice, they were fully prepared. If you're one of those students, I hate to burst your bubble—nothing could be further from the truth. One of the unfortunate byproducts of standardized tests is that students prepare for them and not for college. Unfortunately, some prepare so well that they are admitted to colleges where they find it difficult to compete. If you memorize enough vocabulary to improve your score on the SAT, but—like most students—never really use it, you have a problem. It will be very difficult for you to compete with students who have extensive active vocabularies they use when they write and speak. That is why, if you are wise, you will spend 15 minutes a night reviewing the vocabulary you have just learned. Do this and you will have your newly acquired college-level vocabulary when you arrive on campus. If you allow six to eight months to go by without reviewing, a substantial part of it will slip away.

Colleges insist that the SAT tests your vocabulary because they know it affects your ability to handle complex material. As I mentioned earlier, experience has taught them that students who are verbally impoverished have problems in college and often do not graduate. If you spend as little as 15 minutes a night reviewing and reinforcing what you have learned, your college experience will be richer, more pleasant, and successful.

If you are using flashcards, go through them twice a day for three days each week. If you cannot instantly recall a word or use it in a sentence, read aloud the flashcard for that word a dozen times a day for seven days, slowing down and emphasizing the word each time you say it.

If you are not using the vocabulary flashcards in Part 3, return to Part 1 and read all the definitions, each time trying to recall the word that matches the thought. Then attempt to put that word in a sentence. If you cannot instantly recall a word or use it in a sentence, look it up and put it into a sentence. Read the sentence aloud a dozen times. When you read the word, slow down, emphasize, and write it. Keep doing this until the procedure becomes so boring that you can do it without thinking. This exercise will almost guarantee that you will use your newly acquired vocabulary when you speak and write.

Once you are in college you will be assigned readings containing vocabulary with which you are not familiar. You must not only look up these words, but you also must make a list and study them, using the same techniques I described. Remember, all areas of study have unique vocabularies, and you can't expect to understand a subject until you have mastered its vocabulary.

Once again, good luck!